The Complete Trading System

The Complete Trading System

How to Develop a Mindset, Maximize Profitability, and Own Your Market Success

Casey Stubbs

WILEY

Published by John Wiley & Sons, Inc., Hoboken, New Jersey.
Published simultaneously in Canada.

For general information on our other products and services or for technical support, please contact our Customer Care Department within the United States at (800) 762-2974, outside the United States at (317) 572-3993 or fax (317) 572-4002.

Wiley also publishes its books in a variety of electronic formats. Some content that appears in print may not be available in electronic formats. For more information about Wiley products, visit our web site at www.wiley.com.

Library of Congress Cataloging-in-Publication Data is Available:

ISBN 9781394188123 (Hardback)
ISBN 9781394188109 (ePDF)
ISBN 9781394188116 (ePDF)

Cover Design: Wiley
Cover Image: © Justimagine/Adobe Stock Photos
Author Photo: Courtesy of Casey Stubbs
SKY10086142_092624

I dedicate this book to the Lord Jesus Christ, who rescued me when I didn't deserve it.

Contents

The Complete Trading System

Introduction

I want to begin by thanking you for purchasing this book. It is my sincere desire that you find this to be a valuable tool that will assist you to become a successful trader. I hope to meet many of you who purchase this book. To get the most out of it, I recommend that you contact me and introduce yourself. You can do that by going to my podcast at `https://tradingstrategyguides.com`, listening to an episode, and then reaching out via email.

This book teaches a complete trading system that works in all markets. Once you learn this system, you will be able to make money consistently from the markets.

This book is about trading, and it is not about trading. One of the most important things you need to understand is that trading actually isn't about trading. What I mean is that many of the things I have learned to help me become a better trader are not learned during trading but during other vital areas of my life. For example, recently I began training for my first marathon, during which I learned about proper running form and how to check in with myself every few minutes. What I realized is that the same skill set is critical for trading: proper running form is analogous to taking proper trading setups, and checking in with myself correlates to having a checklist to make sure that I am always taking the right trades.

Such preparation for success is critical in trading, and that preparation to be better in one area of your life will carry over into the next. We are complete human beings, and what we do in our personal life matters in our trading, and what we do in our trading matters in our personal lives.

That is one of the key things I want you to get from this book.

I am going to teach a great strategy that is not taught in any other trading books. However, this book is much more than a strategy. If you bought this book looking for a strategy, be assured that you will get a great strategy, but you will also get so much more. I think you will be surprised at what you will be able to take away from this book when you finish it.

I use many stories outside of trading to illustrate the points I am making. I do this for two reasons:

1. I learned more about trading while doing other things. When I work at raising my family, I learn things that help my trading; when I train for running I learn about trading. When I manage my business, I learn about trading. These lessons outside of trading have helped me become a better trader.
2. Stories hammer the point home, so that you can remember and apply it. These stories and illustrations solidify the lessons I am trying to teach.

As a trader, you should study trading but also have additional hobbies and interests in life and apply the lessons you learn from those things to trading. Remember this: we trade to live, not live to trade.

I wrote this book because I want to get a simple trading strategy in the hands of as many people as possible. Trading is one of the biggest industries in the world. It's the only one where average people like you and I can work from home and make an unlimited amount of money.

Becoming a successful trader is one of the greatest opportunities for building a life with financial security. It is a path to freedom because with financial security you can travel and do things that you want to do.

Be warned though: there are many dangers along the way. Most traders are totally unprepared for what they face when they first start trading. This book will highlight many of those dangers to help you navigate successfully.

This is not a road to getting rich quick. This is a path of small, consistent steps. To grow, you start small. Many times, traders see big dollar signs and believe that this will be an easy road. (I thought this!) It's not. The road will, however, be full of adventure and excitement. And if you choose to walk down this path and do not give up, there's a great reward.

Throughout this book, I share the strategies and tools you need to be a successful trader. I also share my stories and the struggles I had to overcome so you can learn from those and use those lessons as an aid to help you navigate on your own journey to becoming a successful trader.

I also share the stories of the traders I have interviewed on my trading podcast *How To Trade It: Talking with the World's Most Successful Traders* (https://tradingstrategyguides.com/).

I have designed this book with additional resources. There are sections in the book that have a companion video series. The video series would sell for $297. I'm giving it away as a free bonus for everyone that purchases this book.

You can find this free video series titled *The Complete Trading Strategy* at https://tradingstrategyguides.com/book. You will be able to identify these special bonuses because they will look like this note.

When you trade, you are up against some of the smartest and most skilled traders in the world and some of the most expensive equipment and research. The best computer algorithms are competing against the average retail trader, and the challenge is great. And here we are as retail traders. We go out there trying to beat the best of the best. It's like me telling you to suit up with the Pittsburgh Steelers and jump in as the starting quarterback.

I do not tell you to discourage you, I tell you this because I want you to take it seriously and prepare. You can do this if you are willing to do what others are not, and to put in the work to become great.

I look forward to hearing about your future success from learning the complete trading system.

My Personal Introduction to Trading

When I was growing up in the 1980s, my aunt Mary worked for Intel, the computer chip manufacturer. She taught me and my siblings about computers, how to use them and take them apart and put them together. I loved it. It was fun. I wanted to learn everything I could about computers, and playing games was great too.

However, I had no idea that she was teaching me a valuable skill. That skill would be a blessing to me for my entire life, one which I would use going forward. It would help me have great success in trading and in business.

This skill began to help set the path for my trading future. During my teenage years, my dad was very involved in stock trading. He wanted to learn how to trade online, but he didn't really know anything about computers. This was back when online trading just got started. At that time, he asked us to help him get set up trading online. That was in the early nineties. I was about 16 or 17 years old at the time.

When I was teaching my dad how to set up the stock trading system, I got very excited about stocks. That created an instant desire to start trading, and, as a 16-year-old, I envisioned becoming a millionaire trading the markets.

I thought this was going to be easy.

It wasn't exactly easy, but I got a great head start from my family who taught me valuable skills as well as a solid work ethic and strong moral values that guide me today.

This book can be the tool you can use to teach and inspire you to use trading to give success in trading and build a life that gives financial freedom as well.

Part I

Critical Foundations
for Successful Trading

Welcome to the first part of the *Complete Trading System*. This part of the book covers the critical foundations for successful trading, including the trading mindset and understanding how markets work.

In the first chapter, you will discover the importance of having a strong foundation for your trading journey. This includes understanding the importance of having a clear trading mindset and knowing what it takes to be a successful trader.

The second chapter focuses on the trading mindset and the role it plays in determining your success as a trader. You'll learn how to develop a positive and focused mindset, and how to stay disciplined and motivated in the face of challenges.

The third chapter delves into how markets work, including the key concepts and factors that drive market movements. You'll learn about supply and demand, market trends, and other important market dynamics that will help you make informed trading decisions.

By mastering these key concepts, you'll be well on your way to building a complete trading system that will help you achieve your trading goals and maximize your profits.

Chapter 1
The Foundations for Successful Trading

This chapter focuses on the big-picture items and explaining the foundational skills you need to learn as a trader.

Just as with building a house, you must have the proper foundation to be successful as a trader. Without that, your entire endeavor will come crashing down. I know this personally because a house I bought didn't have a good foundation, and the walls caved in and I had to rebuild. I have also had to rebuild my trading skills because some of my habits and ideas were not built on solid methods. I want to make sure you have a solid foundation.

This chapter provides you with the fundamentals you need for success:

- The first thing to know about trading is to keep it simple, so that you will be able to follow and execute the strategy.
- The second thing you need to know about trading is that "simple" doesn't mean it is easy. If it was easy, everyone would be a successful trader.

Trading a Simple System

As I mentioned above, trading is simple; however, you must learn a set of skills that are built one upon another in order to master the craft of trading. In other words, trading is composed of multiple skills that must be put together in order for you to be successful.

I like to compare trading skills to the human body. The human body has a lot of different moving parts. We have a brain. We have a skeletal system. We have a muscular system. We have a nervous system. All of these things work together to create a healthy functioning human body.

If one of those systems is out of place, it messes up everything else in the body. For example, if your skeletal system is weak, you'll break bones, and it's going to ruin your quality of life. All the systems of the body need to be working properly. And trading is the same way. There are many foundational things that you need to learn and apply to be successful.

Many traders think if they just learn a strategy, that's all they need to know. But there are many different skills that you need to learn in addition to strategy.

This book is written to teach one key skill at a time. Then, I put the entire system together to come up with a way to be successful in trading. Because just as the human body works as a complete system, when trading, if we don't have all systems functioning properly, the entire trading will not be as profitable as it could be.

We must focus on one skill at a time as we learn to become a winning trader. Focus is one skill that a trader must develop to truly excel at trading.

Here are each of the foundations that you will learn and apply by the end of this book.

1. Trading mindset.
2. How to complete a market analysis.
3. Identifying trends a trading them for maximum market movement.
4. Market flow and levels. Learn how to be better than bank traders by understanding these.
5. Candlestick patterns and chart patterns: increase your accuracy with these patterns.
6. How to form a daily trade plan.
7. High-performance entry methods.
8. Using a daily process to create high performance and consistency.
9. Risk management execution and strategy.
10. Road map for long-term growth.
11. Profit maximizers to compound your trading profits with investing.

Once you put all this together and learn this system, you will have a way to create extra revenue for the rest of your life.

The Power of Consistency

One of the major themes of this book, which does not get discussed often, is the power of *consistency*.

Before you can make $1 million you need to know how to make $1 and then keep $1. Then you need to know how to do it again, and again. Each day. Every day.

Many people think they are wasting their time learning to make $1, but the truth is that if you can learn to make $1 consistently, then you can learn to make $10 consistently. And from there you can learn to make thousands of dollars in the market.

But it is a process, and it starts small. John Meli—one of my students, friends, and now coach who works for my trading education company, Trading Strategy Guides—often says that the "market is designed to take money from you."

He is right, but those of us who learn to *keep* it consistently can become consistently successful traders.

Do not look at your (potential) millions before you learn to make $1. Once you learn to make small amounts of money, you can learn to make large amounts of money. I like to focus on the big picture just like everyone else, but it is important to realize we need to start small and work our way up to massive trading success.

The best way to be a successful trader is to start small. Learn how to consistently take profits out of the market, and if you can do that, then you can scale up later on if you want to.

Shortcuts will not work for trading success. If you want to solve your financial problems with trading, that is a noble thing to do; however, you must know that there are no shortcuts. You must learn the key foundational aspects of trading that I lay out for you step by step in this book.

Next, I talk about major obstacles to trading success.

Biggest Obstacles to Success

There are many things that will snag you along the way. These obstacles are not always obvious, so I'm laying it out here in the first chapter. These are the main major obstacles that I have experienced:

1. Believing that all I need is a strategy and disregarding the rest of the foundations.

2. Not following a system—because of lack of discipline and trying to make money too fast.
3. Not taking responsibility for success—blaming the markets or others for my mistakes.
4. Risk management issues—not being careful with risk, trying to get rich quick by risking big.
5. Quitting before breakthrough. There are so many times I stopped too soon. If I had just kept at it a bit longer, I would have been successful.
6. Having a too-complicated system. It is very difficult to follow a complicated system, so we are going to keep things simple.
7. System hopping—jumping from system to system because I think that is the answer when my own lack of integrity is what has caused me to fail.

Richard Dennis, the founder of the Turtle Traders, once said that you can publish the rules of the strategy, and because people have no discipline, they will not follow them. I have concrete proof that this is a true statement. An example of this is that my website TradingStrategyGuides.com has hundreds of free trading strategies. I have people going to that site every day to learn how to trade the markets. Yet few learn and are successful as a result of their searching—even though there are hundreds of strategies posted for free.

The reason most people struggle to learn successful trading is because trading isn't as easy as they hope it will be. When things are difficult, you must dive down, dig deep, and figure out how to solve the problem in front of you.

People tend to jump from strategy to strategy, looking for the next big thing. One reason my website (TradingStrategyGuides .com) is so popular is that I offer many strategies for free. Many of the traders who get these free strategies will later update to paid strategies. They do this not because the paid strategies are better.

The main reason is that some traders lack the discipline to follow a strategy consistently.

There is a serious condition called the *shiny object syndrome*. People with this syndrome will try 100 different strategies, but they won't master any of them. This is something I suffered with until I learned the hard way. By failing so many times, the pain became too great, and I finally just changed—I learned that there is no reason to switch to a new system if you're not properly trading the one you have.

Rather than work to solve the real problem, people with this syndrome will jump from new thing to new thing, getting only a surface level of understanding. My pastor, Doug Allen, often says "that many times people have knowledge about many things, but that understanding is only an inch deep. To have true understanding, we must dive in deep on a few things."

To become a master, we must work on a set of things over and over again until we master it. If you as a trader continue to switch strategies because you haven't found one that works, I am warning you right now it is not the strategy that doesn't work.

The problem is that you are not trading the strategy properly.

Not Following a Strategy

If you do not consistently trade the same way, you are not following your strategy. One thing I teach, to help you evaluate your trading strategy, is to look at your last 20 trades and analyze them. (You will be learning this important skill later on, in the daily trading process section of the book.) If you were not profitable, what was the cause?

Was it any of the following?

1. The strategy was followed perfectly, and it was a loser.
2. You lost because you didn't follow entry criteria (a set of rules that a trader must follow when entering a trade).

3. You lost because you didn't follow risk (the set amount of money that a trader is willing to risk on any given trade).
4. You have no idea what happened because you didn't review your trades and you're guessing about the success or failure of the trades.

From personal experience and in teaching others, I will tell you that most of the people will be guilty of item 4. Most do not have any idea what they are doing or what works—they are completely shooting from the hip.

If you do happen to take the time to review and analyze your trades, you will notice that items 2 or 3 were probably the reason that you didn't make money. That is easy to fix: in the next set of 20 trades, make sure you correctly identify entry points and risk management criteria, and then try again.

Keep doing this process repeatedly, until you are following proper risk and entry criteria.

If you look at the above list of four points and find that you did everything correctly and you still lost money, congratulations! This puts you in the top 1%! Very few people can follow a strategy exactly as it has been designed to be traded.

This outcome (losing money), however, is easy to fix because now all you must do is adjust one set of criteria for the next set of 20 trades, until you find a winner.

I will be laying out a great strategy for you to begin your testing in this book. The point I am trying to get across now is that this is a key obstacle. If you can identify this now, you will have a huge advantage in your journey to becoming a successful trader.

Remember there is no holy grail strategy.

It is important to find one strategy and continue to trade it and tweak it and make it work. Each strategy becomes unique to the trader trading. We all see things differently, and we must do the work necessary to make the strategy work for us.

When you're learning to trade, you need to look into the mirror. Realize that the problem you're having in your trading is not your strategy. It's that person looking back at you in the mirror. If you want to be successful, understand that you are the reason for success or failure. It's not your strategy.

In the mindset training that you'll learn later in this book, I focus a lot on self-sabotage. The person in the mirror. You can either be your greatest enemy or your greatest ally. And I find that most traders who are not successful have the element of self-sabotage in their life.

Not Taking Responsibility for Success or Failure

When you look in the mirror, you must understand that you are the one taking the trades. Don't be someone who blames others and doesn't take responsibility for their own failure.

Losing traders blame the markets. They blame the strategy; they blame the news that just came out. They blame the indicator they are using or the trainer who is teaching them the markets. They blame everyone but themselves for failure. It's important to realize that successful people take ownership for success and failure. And that it comes down to themselves.

I didn't become successful in trading until I took ownership over the results of my trading. And that meant doing whatever it took to be successful. That meant going to the training classes, learning to have a great trading mindset, learning the systems, learning how to have proper discipline. Talking to people who could help me. Sharing my struggles in trading and being responsible for my undisciplined approach to trading. I tackled all these problems one at a time until I built up my consistency and discipline.

If you are not ready to take responsibility, you are just wasting your time and racking up losses, which will in turn destroy your psychological ability to have success in the markets.

Risk Management Failure

Successful trading is all about managing risk. Managing risk is simply being a good financial manager.

This is as simple as learning how to manage your own personal finances. Do you spend more money than you make?

Are you in massive debt or in financial hardship?

Trading from a Weak Financial Position

On my show, the *How To Trade It* podcast, I find out about the background of many of the traders and why they started trading. Here is a common theme for the ones that end in failure: a trader has a financial problem, and they need money, and they discover trading and believe it can solve that financial problem.

In contrast, successful traders are people who are financially in great shape and use trading to continue to add to their good financial position.

I have found, across the board, that people in a healthy financial position who start trading are much more likely to be successful traders than those who are in a dire situation.

I recently interviewed Sunny Harris, a 42-year veteran trader from moneymentor.com, on the *How To Trade It* podcast. Her company was bought out, giving her a windfall. She started trading because she believed she could do much better by trading than by entrusting her wealth to money managers. She was right, and she became an extremely successful trader. However, she didn't come from a weak financial position.

Traders who need money face several problems. If this describes you, you need to be aware of the following.

1. Trading is a financial problem you need to solve, not a lottery or get-rich-quick scenario.

2. Trading when you're in financial distress puts added pressure on you to perform, which is not conducive to trading success.
3. Trading can also be an addiction and an escape mechanism, just like alcoholism. Sometimes traders will trade just for the thrill of having money on the line.

Money comes to people who solve problems for themselves and others. Money comes to people who add value to the world.

Trading is a wonderful thing to learn and master. Just go in knowing that it is a difficult problem you will need to solve, not a get-rich-quick end to your financial pain.

There is no quick solution to getting out of a bad financial situation. For example, studies show that most people who win the lottery end up in a worse financial situation after they win the big prize than before they won.[1]

The problem is we need money now, and we want money now. The market can solve that problem fast. However, the market will not reward us with success until we deserve it by executing a strategy—with an edge, with discipline, consistently.

When we try to use the market as a shortcut to financial success, it makes our financial condition terrible. We are in even worse shape by pouring more money into our trading account.

Patrick Reid, the co-founder of the Adamis Principle and a guest of mine on *How To Trade It,* suggests that traders give themselves a cutoff point—a point where they stop trading if they can't make it past the cutoff point. If you have a $10,000 account, choose, say, 20% ($2,000) as the maximum amount of loss you will tolerate. If you exceed that, you should stop trading. That gives you plenty of time to learn how to trade effectively and stops you from putting money into a losing investment.

Gambling Instead of Trading

Many years ago, I saw someone in a casino lose all their money at the slot machine. They took money out of an ATM, then lost all of that too, repeating this cycle until their bank account was empty. If you are not able to figure out why you are losing money, just stop and reassess until you are able to figure things out.

When you think that trading will solve your problems, but you don't put the work in, all you are doing is gambling, hoping to find that shortcut to success. That mindset is destructive and addictive; you're just gambling, and gamblers never win. When my trading students are gambling in the markets I explain that successful trading is taking calculated and well-planned risks.

Make sure you put the time and effort into learning how to be a successful trader. In the long term, the rewards will be worth the time that you put into learning how to trade.

The Science of Addiction

Our brains release a chemical called dopamine as a reward for doing something good. This can be triggered when you take a trade, when you win a trade, but also when you lose a trade. This is very addictive, and it is why it can be so difficult to close losing trades. This is also why many times traders will continue to trade over and over again.[2]

Dopamine is the same chemical that gets released when you eat food and celebrate wins. While this is great for helping you develop good habits, it is equally destructive when you have to fight the bad habits.

Instant gratification becomes addictive because of dopamine. As technology increases, we get addicted to things moving faster and faster in our lives. For example, interactions on social media platforms like Facebook, Twitter, and TikTok are so addictive because you generally get feedback almost instantly, and each exchange is usually of very short duration. It is important for traders to understand that this is something they need to be aware of, and they need to make sure that they are not addicted to trading—and if you are, you need to put in place a plan to stop the addiction.

Most traders who get addicted to trading replenish trading account after trading account. People can even lose jobs, homes, and relationships because of the trading addiction.

If you find yourself obsessed with trading, putting all your time and energy into trading, this is one of the first signs that you might have a problem. Some signs that can help you be aware of this are:

- Anger at your trading losses
- Problems with relationships because of trading
- Losing too much money, causing financial problems
- Borrowing money to help cover your trading losses

Revenge Trading

When you lose money trading and then all you can think about is making that money back and making bigger trades and trading more frequently, this is called *revenge trading*. When you combine this with addiction and dopamine, it is a disaster waiting to happen.

If you find yourself in this position, be aware of what is going on and just stop trading. Then come up with a plan to get back into the markets later on when you are ready to trade and be in control of yourself and not let your addictive nature be in charge.

Only trade with money that you can afford to lose. Do not trade with money you will need to pay bills. There is no shame in reaching out for help. Determine that you are going to make a change in your life. Next, make a plan for how you are going to change—then execute.

If you need to get help, find a support system to help you with your problem.

The true trader focuses on the process of mastering trading, not on making their money back fast or getting rich quickly. As Mark Yegge said on the *How to Trade It* podcast: "The way to get rich fast is to get rich slow."[3]

Quitting Before Having a Breakthrough

I believe that anyone can trade, yet the failure rate is about 99.9% for day traders—not encouraging numbers.

When faced with failure, many traders will say that trading isn't for them, or they quit. But in most cases they never gave it a great shot because they didn't follow their system properly and didn't use proper trade management. Aim to continue to improve little by little each day, and if you do not quit, you will eventually find trading success.

One story that has inspired me greatly was that of my friend Tony Pawlak from Real Life Trading. Tony told me when I interviewed him on my podcast that he had spent $60,000 of his personal savings in trading losses. Plus he added an additional $80,000 in debt trying to become a successful trader.

He kept going and kept working at it until now he is a successful, profitable trader.

While I do not recommend going down $140,000 of your own money, he inspired me to understand that if you do not give up you will eventually do what it takes to learn this craft of trading.[4]

Summary

In this chapter, I discuss the foundations of trading: a solid trading plan, discipline, proper risk management, and ongoing education and learning. I emphasize that having a well-defined and written trading plan is essential for my success in trading, as it provides a clear roadmap for making decisions and staying focused. Discipline is also crucial for me, as it allows me to stick to my plan and avoid emotional trading. Risk management is also important to protect against losses, and ongoing education and learning are necessary for me to stay informed and adapt to changing market conditions.

I also highlight several major obstacles that I face as a trader, including lack of discipline, poor risk management, lack of a solid trading plan, emotional trading, and lack of education or experience. I note that these obstacles can lead me to make impulsive and uninformed decisions, which can result in significant losses. I also stress that realistic expectations and patience are important for me, as becoming a successful trader takes time and effort. Additionally, I should also note that the financial markets are uncertain, and even with my experience, I can experience losses.

I conclude by emphasizing that by focusing on the four foundations of trading and addressing the major obstacles, I can increase my chances of success in the markets.

This book will give you all the tools you will need to be successful in the trading market.

Notes

1. https://direct.mit.edu/rest/article-abstract/93/3/961/57969/The-Ticket-to-Easy-Street-The-Financial?redirectedFrom=fulltext.
2. https://www.responsiblegambling.org/for-the-public/about-gambling/the-science-behind-gambling/#:~:text=When%20you%20gamble%2C%20your%20brain,response%20even%20when%20you%20lose.
3. https://podcast.tradingstrategyguides.com/the-fast-way-to-make-money-with-mark-yegge-ep-131/.
4. https://podcast.tradingstrategyguides.com/90-win-rate-by-trading-credit-spreads-with-tony-pawlak/.

Chapter 2

Mindset: Developing the Mental Game to Dominate in the Markets

This chapter is about "mindset" and how you can develop yours in a way that can help you avoid the obstacles I mentioned in Chapter 1. Over the years, I've talked with hundreds of successful traders on my podcast, and the number-one reason for trading failure is this: traders do not focus on their mental game. This chapter will give you the strategies for creating a winning mindset.

The key elements needed to create a winning trading mindset are:

1. Committing to the process
2. Believing in your eventual success
3. Taking responsibility for your trading

4. Developing a mindset of integrity
5. Controlling what you can and releasing the rest
6. Developing good habits
7. Planning for failure
8. Knowing how and why to keep a trading journal
9. Study and self-education

This chapter explains in detail these nine steps to creating a winning mindset.

In our journey to becoming a successful trader, we must first focus on mindset because if you do not have a well-disciplined mind, you will allow self-sabotage to get in, and that can derail you from becoming the trader that you desire to be.

Commitment to Trading Success

Before you begin your trading journey, you must understand that there is a great commitment that will be required to eventually find success. The best way to give yourself the best opportunity to make a commitment is to do a cost vs. rewards analysis. It is important that you evaluate the costs versus the potential rewards. When you have evaluated the cost versus rewards, you can make a decision you can commit to.

Evaluating costs versus potential rewards involves comparing the costs of a project or decision to the potential benefits that can be gained from it. The process can be broken down into the following steps:

1. Identify the costs: These include monetary costs, time costs, risk costs, opportunity costs, environmental and social costs, and future costs, as mentioned in the previous answer.
2. Identify the potential rewards: These include the tangible and intangible benefits of the project or decision, such as

increased revenue, improved efficiency, or positive social or environmental impact.

3. Compare the costs and rewards: This can be done by creating a cost-benefit analysis, which involves creating a list of costs and rewards and assigning a value to each. The costs and rewards can then be compared to determine the overall value of the project or decision.

4. Make a decision: After evaluating the costs and rewards, you can make a decision about whether to proceed with the project or decision. If the potential rewards outweigh the costs, the project or decision may be considered viable. If the costs outweigh the potential rewards, it may not be worth pursuing.

When they first start trading, many traders do not understand the cost of becoming successful. The very first thing you should do is evaluate whether or not you are willing to pay the price of this journey to becoming a trader. The following list outlines the "costs" that I will talk about in the following sections to help you in your decision-making process. This is not an exhaustive list, but it gives you the ability to make a solid decision.

1. Time cost
2. Educational cost
3. Capital cost

Time Cost

It is going to take hours and hours of time working at this to become an expert at trading.

Malcolm Gladwell is an author and journalist who has written several books, including *Outliers: The Story of Success*, in which he discusses the concept of "the 10,000-hour rule."

The rule states that it takes roughly 10,000 hours of practice to become an expert in a particular field. Gladwell suggests that individuals who have achieved exceptional success in their respective fields have typically put in this amount of time, either through deliberate practice or through a combination of natural talent and opportunity. The idea is that reaching that level of practice or experience is a key factor in achieving mastery in a particular field.[1]

One example of the 10,000-hour rule discussed in *Outliers* is the story of the Beatles. Gladwell states that the Beatles, before they became famous, played for thousands of hours in Hamburg, Germany, in the early 1960s. They played for several hours a night, almost every night, for several months at a time. By the time they had their first hit in 1964, they had already logged thousands of hours of performance time. Gladwell argues that this extensive practice and performing experience was a significant factor in their success as musicians and in their rise to fame.

In trading, the 10,000-hour rule can be applied similarly to how it applies to other fields. A trader who wants to become an expert in a particular market or strategy would need to put in a significant amount of time and practice. This could include studying market trends and historical data, testing and refining trading strategies, and actually executing trades in a simulated or live environment. Over time, as a trader logs more and more hours in the market and gains more experience, they may become more proficient and successful in their trading.

It's important to note that while the 10,000-hour rule may provide a general idea of the amount of time and practice required to become an expert in a field, it is not a guarantee of success. Trading is a complex and dynamic field, and many other factors such as risk management, emotional control, and market knowledge are also important for success. Additionally, the 10,000-hour rule is not a magic number; it is more of a general framework.

Achieving 10,000 hours of practice and experience in trading may require a significant commitment of time and energy. However, it is important to balance this with other aspects of life, such as family, friends, and personal health and well-being.

It is possible for a trader to become proficient and successful in the market while still maintaining a healthy work–life balance. This could involve setting specific goals and a schedule for studying and practicing trading, as well as taking regular breaks and time off to focus on other areas of life.

Additionally, it's important to mention that the 10,000 hours is not a hard-and-fast rule, and one can achieve mastery at a much lower number of hours as well. It depends on the individual, their natural talents, and how much time they can dedicate to the task they are trying to learn each day. It's important to remember that the number of hours is not the only thing that matters; the quality of the practice is also very important.

Educational Cost

You will have to invest in education, whether it is learning from YouTube or learning by signing up for educational courses.

Some examples include:

- **Tuition costs:** Many traders take formal education courses such as a degree in finance, economics or business administration, or specialized trading courses.
- **Books and materials:** Traders may need to purchase books, online courses, or other materials to learn about the markets, trading strategies, and risk management techniques.
- **Software and technology costs:** Traders may need to purchase or subscribe to trading software, charting platforms, and other technology to help with their analysis and decision making.

- **Mentoring and coaching costs:** Some traders may choose to work with a mentor or coach to help them improve their trading skills and strategies.
- **Trading simulation costs:** Traders may need to invest in trading simulation software or services to practice their skills in a risk-free environment.
- **Data and research costs:** Traders may need to subscribe to financial data and research services to stay informed about the markets and the companies they trade.

It's important to note that these costs can vary widely depending on the trader's goals and the resources available to them. Some of the costs may be substantial, and traders should be prepared to invest in their education in order to improve their chances of success.

Capital Cost

You must accurately understand that there is financial capital that is required to be able to trade. The amount of capital needed to start trading successfully can vary depending on the individual trader and their goals. However, in general, it is recommended to have a significant amount of capital when starting out as a trader.

For day trading, which is a strategy that involves buying and selling positions within a single trading day, the minimum recommended capital is around $25,000 to $30,000. This is based on the *pattern day trader* rule, which states that a trader must have at least $25,000 in their account to day trade in the United States.

For swing trading, which is a strategy that involves holding positions for a few days to a few weeks, the minimum recommended capital can be lower than for day trading, but it depends on the trader's risk management and position size.

For long-term trading, which is a strategy that involves holding positions for several months or years, the minimum recommended capital can be lower, but it also depends on the trader's goals and risk tolerance.

It's important to note that having a larger amount of capital can provide more flexibility and a larger margin for error. Additionally, the amount of capital needed can vary depending on the specific markets and instruments being traded as well as the trader's level of experience and knowledge.

It's also important to be aware that trading can be risky, and it's possible to lose all or a significant portion of your capital.

One important tip is that you do not need to have a lot of capital to get started because you must first learn to trade successfully before needing a large amount of capital. Focus on consistency first, then capital second. Start small, then grow your account or apply for funds through prop trading.

It is much easier to get capital for trading now with prop firms that will provide the funds for you to trade, such as the trading strategy guides prop firm.[2]

Now that we have looked at the costs, we must weigh those against potential rewards. There are several potential rewards for someone who becomes a successful trader. Some of these include:

- **Financial rewards:** Successful traders can earn significant income through trading profits and commissions.
- **Career advancement:** A successful trader may have the opportunity to advance to a more senior role, such as a portfolio manager or trading desk head.

- **Freedom and flexibility:** Many traders have the ability to work independently and set their own schedules, which can provide a high degree of flexibility.
- **Challenge and excitement:** Trading can be a challenging and exciting field, and successful traders may find a great deal of satisfaction from being able to navigate the markets and make profitable trades.
- **Independence:** Successful traders can also have the opportunity to be self-employed, becoming their own boss and making their own trading strategies.
- **Learning opportunities:** Trading can be a challenging field, and successful traders will have the opportunity to constantly learn and adapt to the markets.
- **Networking opportunities:** Successful traders may also have the opportunity to network with other traders and professionals in the financial industry.

It's important to note that while the potential rewards of becoming a successful trader can be significant, the field is also highly competitive and risky. Becoming a successful trader requires a great deal of hard work, dedication, and knowledge of the markets, as well as the ability to manage risk and adapt to changing market conditions.

The journey begins with a decision to commit to the process to become a successful trader. This first step is the one that will give you the ability to create the successful trading mindset that we are going to be discussing in the rest of this chapter.

If you do not quit, you will succeed. I encourage you to make the commitment to start on this journey—it is worth the effort.

Believe in Your Eventual Success

Why would you start to trade if you don't believe that you can achieve success? Perhaps you believe in your eventual success when you start, but chasing success gets too hard along the way, and you lose your faith.

To achieve any difficult task you must first believe that you will ultimately prevail in every endeavor that you seek to achieve.

A famous quote from the *Bible* about faith is a truth that can also be applied to trading.

> Jesus replied, "Truly I tell you, if you have faith as small as a mustard seed, you can say to this mountain, 'Move from here to there,' and it will move. Nothing will be impossible for you."
>
> *Matthew 17:20–21 NASB*

Trading is hard, and it will test you because of the ups and downs you will face as you learn this skill.

Admiral James B. Stockdale was a prisoner of war during the Vietnam War for seven years. During his time in prison many of those who were incarcerated with him died before they could be released.

Stockdale was quoted as saying that the optimists were the ones who died first. They would say *I will be out of here by Christmas*. Then when that didn't happen, they were defeated and discouraged. Then they would say *I will be out of here by Easter*, and then when that didn't happen, they would be defeated and discouraged.

He calls them optimists because they thought release was going to come easy or quickly.

He had a strong belief that he was going be released despite his terrible circumstances. During this time, he developed a mindset that later became known as the Stockdale principle. He said:

> "You must never confuse faith that you will prevail in the end, which you can never afford to lose, with the discipline to confront the most brutal facts of your current reality whatever they may be."[3]

This is extremely useful when we run into the problems that will come to us during our trading career. I have tried to adopt this not only in my own life in trading but also in every other obstacle that I have faced and will face. Two important principles are:

1. Face brutal reality: If we are losing money trading or we are not following our rules, we must confront the fact that we are failing. You know things are not working out because your account balance is decreasing. Own it and address it:

   Yes, right now we are losing, and right now we do not have the skills we need to trade successfully. However, I will make changes to adjust to ensure that I will accomplish my trading goals.

2. Discouragement will set in when failure comes; however, we can combat that by having complete faith that we will overcome no matter how difficult it is. Do not put a time limit on your success, focus on the process and focus on your trading, and work each and every day to get better. But do not put a time limit on this process, because if you keep at it, you will overcome your obstacles.

   Do not believe that it will be easy, but instead believe that you know it will be difficult but that you will have success. Then when it gets hard, you will not allow that discouragement to cause you to quit.

   A quote by Jim Rohn that I think of often is "Don't wish it was easier, wish you were better. Don't wish for less problems, wish for more skills. Don't wish for less challenge, wish for more wisdom."[4]

This understanding of mindset has helped me have the endurance and perseverance to become a successful trader, and if you adopt this mindset, it will give you what you need to become successful as well.

Taking Responsibility for the Outcome Is Critical

Responsibility is a superpower that most people do not know how to activate in their lives. I recently was having a deep discussion about responsibility with my friend Markus Neukom, a leadership expert, and he explained to me in simple terms that responsibility is simply the ability to respond to something. One reason I call responsibility a superpower is because those who choose to take ownership get a sense of purpose, which carries a great deal of authority in our lives. People who have purpose are living for something greater. This purpose can carry you through incredible adversity and challenges.

Human beings were created for a purpose, and it is important for each person to find theirs. Trading is great for making money, but what is your purpose? Why are you trading? What is the end result that you want to accomplish with your trading? Knowing your purpose will give you an additional tool to help in your trading journey.

You have the ability to respond to all of your trading challenges if you choose to. The way that you respond as a trader will contribute to how you develop as a trader.

When difficult trading challenges come your way, there are common ways to respond to them.

1. Find a new tool or strategy.
2. Keep trading and hope it will go away (or essentially no response).
3. Face the difficulty, study it, and respond directly to the problem.

The first item in this list—finding a new tool or strategy—is a superficial way of solving the problem, because you are not actually addressing the root of the problem. If you try to solve your problems in this way, you will not be able to find true issues because you are not going deep enough to get an understanding of how you need to change to be a successful trader. There are many traders that are always finding new tools, and they will continue to do so for years and never go deep enough to get the skills needed for success.

The next one is the hope strategy. I have heard it said many times that hope is not a strategy, and I agree. If you are failing and you continue to trade without taking drastic action to figure out the source of the problem, you are just hoping, and that is how traders will continue to trade their accounts into the ground.

The best response is to face the difficulty—analyze it and come up with a plan to prevent the behavior that is causing you to lose or not trade well. If you adopt this response to your poor trading, you will become a champion trader.

Facing your problems head on and working on a solution—this is how greatness happens. It is rare in the world, but I believe that you can do it!

Developing a Mindset of Integrity

This quality is one of the best character traits we can develop to help us maintain discipline and become great traders.

Integrity is a big factor in trading success.

Integrity is when you keep your word. You do what you say you are going to do. Or doing the right thing all the time because it is the right thing to do.

How do you know what the right thing is? It is having a code of values, and you must define those values. Most people today are not walking with integrity because they have not taken the time to define their values. Take the time to find out what is right, develop your values, and have a clear code to live by.

What would those values be as a trader?

They would be creating a trading plan and following the defined rules of that plan. If you do not make a plan, you will not have any values to uphold. Yet we see that most failed traders do not take the time to do this and therefore lose massively and embarrassingly in the markets.

One other key point I want to make about integrity is keeping your word. Sticking to your values means keeping your word.

I often say that it is easy to keep your word to other people because there is a consequence to a lack of integrity. For example, if you promise to do a report in your job, and you do not keep your word, the consequence is that people will call you unreliable, and you will not keep that job very long!

However, the harder part of having integrity is keeping your word to yourself. The reason keeping your word to yourself can be so difficult is that you are the only one who knows that you are breaking your word, so there are not any immediate consequences.

There are dire consequences for not keeping your word to yourself, but you are not held accountable to the world because no one knows but you.

We might make a promise to ourselves to not eat any cookies, yet when you go to Grandma's house, she has an entire bowl and you end up eating the entire thing. At the end of the day, that might not be a big deal, but over time it adds up, and every time you fail to keep your word to yourself you become weaker and weaker, and it gets harder and harder to maintain those boundaries to have a solid level of integrity.

In trading we may say that we set a limit to only lose $10 on a trade, but we end up losing $100. That is not having integrity. If you say that you are going to do something and you do not do it, you will never be a successful trader.

A trader must have as high a level of integrity as possible. This is something I specifically track and measure. Each day I have a daily trade plan and a daily risk plan. I keep track each day on how well

I follow my plan. Yes, I track my results, my wins and losses, and how much money I make, but more important to me is whether I followed my plan and demonstrated the highest level of integrity.

Practice keeping your word to yourself. You will be a better trader, and it will carry over from trading into other areas of your life, and you will be amazed at how important this is and how you will see your life improve.

One way to help yourself with integrity is to hold yourself accountable. You are ultimately the only person who will be responsible for your integrity, and it is critical that you have a standard in this area of your life and hold yourself to it.

One tool that can help is to find someone in your life to help you be accountable. This could be anyone, from a trading friend to a professional trading coach or life coach. If no matter what you do, you cannot seem to stick to your plan, then finding someone who can look over your trades and trading decisions might be the step you need to take to help you with this.

Remember, you are responsible, and you need to do what it takes to be successful, and if this is what you need to do, then do it.

Being transparent with someone can also help with mindset because if you make some mistakes and you can share that with someone else in your life, that can help you correct your unprofitable behaviors and bad habits.

Keeping those emotions bottled up without a way of releasing them can be a recipe for disaster. One way to release these emotions is on social media or by finding an online trading community. However, I must warn you that finding the right person to share with can be a challenge because if you watch the Twitter feeds online, the traders make it appear as if there are only winners and no losers.

This is because people love to share their wins and hate to share their losses. If you do get an accountability partner in your trading, make sure you are truly transparent and share both the good and the bad, the wins and the losses. I did an entire episode on the *How to Trade It* podcast on this topic titled "Destroy the Biggest Obstacle to Trading Success in One Step with Casey Stubbs, Ep #123."[5]

Control Is an Illusion

There are few things that we can control. We don't control the time that we were born, we do not control what gender we were born as. We do not control who our parents were. We cannot control what happens to us in our lives. We cannot control the markets, nor can we control whether we win or lose a trade after we enter it.

Continuing on the theme of responsibility discussed earlier in this chapter, while we cannot control what happens to us, we can control how we respond. We can choose to get totally unhinged and go crazy, or we can have a calm and rational response.

Viktor Frankl was an Austrian-born neurologist, psychiatrist, and philosopher who was thrown into a German concentration camp in 1942 with his family—where his father, mother, and wife were killed, and he was the only one who survived.

He was quoted as saying, "Forces beyond your control can take away everything you possess except one thing, your freedom to choose how you will respond to the situation."[6]

This is one of the most extreme possible situations, and yet Frankl chose to respond by maintaining his purpose during this time.

One of the key factors that helped him make healthy mental choices in the midst of terrible life circumstances was his sense of purpose that he still had a great deal of things to do.

If we have that sense of purpose in our lives, it will help us make better choices. One thing that has helped me to continue to pursue trading success and not quit is that I have a purpose much bigger than trading. This purpose keeps me on the path to make those choices.

Remember that we cannot control the market.

Here is what we can control:

1. When we get into the market
2. When we get out of the market
3. How much risk we have
4. How we respond after we enter a trade

With each of these points we must maximize our efforts and not allow fear or greed or any other emotions to cause us to lose control of our original plans.

Because it is easy to forget that we have total control of our actions, this is why preparation is so important, because the more we review our trades and strategy the less we will be likely to allow outside forces to cause us to deviate from our plan and make decisions that are disastrous for our trading careers. Remember, one mistake can cancel a great trading career.

Creating Good Habits for Long-Term Trading Success

One way to ensure that we have a rock-solid all-star mindset that will guarantee becoming a winning trader is to create good habits. There is an old saying that we are creatures of habit, and this is true. However, the key is that we have habits that build success or habits that drive us to failure.

Everyone has bad habits, and in trading these bad habits are one of the most important reasons that we see such a high failure rate for new traders.

We can program ourselves to be effective in life if we purposely build good habits. Recently I read *Atomic Habits* by James Clear.[7] He shares in detail how to build great habits that can change your life.

I have added a summary of some of his key points below because I have adopted some of these in my life and for trading.

1. Small habits can have a massive impact on your life. This is not something that you may realize, but over time these small habits add up and lead to great gains.
2. Habits are automated behaviors in our lives, sort of like a computer program, and it is up to us to set the programming so that we can get maximum benefit.
3. Add clear reminders that will be impossible to miss such as putting your running shoes on the kitchen table to remind you to run each day.
4. We are motivated by rewards, so give yourself small rewards to help you stick with your new habit. Yes, the behaviors are automatic behaviors; however, we must program ourselves, and the habits don't easily stick unless we have them fully ingrained in us.
5. If you want to have a new habit, then make it as easy as possible and remove obstacles that could stop you from building the habit.
6. Make it so that you get quick satisfaction to help you continue with the excitement of your new habit.
7. Find a way to measure success—what is measured is what gets done.

It is important for traders to understand which habits can help us and which habits can cause us to fail.

The following is a list of seven habits that you could consider developing that will help you become a profitable trader. These habits will help you build discipline, which is essential to grow your trading account.

1. Have a well-established trading plan with clear rules that are easy to follow.
2. Have a daily trading routine where you follow the same steps every day.
3. Have a clearly defined risk management plan.
4. Have a strategy for removing profit from your broker account to your personal account.
5. Have a strategy for experiencing emotion so that emotions will not cause you to make bad decisions.
6. Have a daily, weekly, and monthly review process that helps to evaluate performance.
7. Create a strong habit to know when you should stop trading.

Once you build these habits, you will begin to see a massive difference in your trading. Once you learn how to create good habits, you can continue to build additional good habits, a process that is known as habit stacking. This is the secret that ultra-successful people use to get massive results in life.

Make a Plan for When You Fail

With trading you are guaranteed to lose trades and have periods of drawdown. We must be mentally ready for when those times come.

Similar to baseball players—who most of the time are not successful at bat, you will fail as a trader, and you will fail often. This is something that cannot be avoided. After all, a highly successful baseball player has an average of only .300, which means that they fail about 70% of the time. You must have a plan to help you deal with that failure.

The first step to having a good plan for failure is awareness. That means understanding that you will fail and being ready for it when it happens. There is a great deal of information on social media and YouTube showing traders who make money every day or have massively high win rates.

This type of media can cause us to have an unrealistic expectation about what we should be expecting on a daily basis with our trading.

Once you understand that you will have many failing trades and days, you must have a plan for how to deal with those losses. One of the reasons this is important is that losses can cause us psychological damage, and that can send us into a tailspin or trading slump. Having a plan to stop those slumps before they get going can be the difference between being a winning and losing trader.

Here are some plans I have developed that have helped me turn my losing days into winning days. These are deliberate action steps that I take when I fail to turn things around.

1. When I am day trading, after each trade I take a break. I step away from the computer, grab some water, do 15 pushups and situps, and then get back to the screen. This helps me reset my mind and get fresh. Plus this helps me get some healthy habits for my body as well as exercise, and water is good for the body and mind.

2. If I lose three trades in a row, I stop for the day. I then review those trades and see why I was off. Sometimes we don't see things the way we should, and if we take a break, it can help us get momentum for the next day. I learned about these three trade rules during an interview I conducted with Michael Patak from Top Step Trader.[8] When I have a losing

day, I want it to be small, so that when I come back I can come back fast.

3. When I have two losing days in a row, I reduce my trade size by 50%. That way I stop losing, so I do not dig a massive hole that I need to climb out of. Mentally a huge drawdown can have a terrible effect on your trading.

Coming up with this process was something I incorporated when reading an article from Lance Beggs.[9] Lance is a great trading coach who has helped me stay focused on being strategic in my trading.

This has helped keep me from following up with more risky trades, which can create a losing spiral that can be very difficult to get out of.

I encourage you to prepare yourself for these failures before they happen, and have your own plan to help you. Remember, one failure can lead to another, and that can send you into a death spiral that can end your career.

The Benefits of a Trading Journal

Maintaining a trading journal will be valuable for you as a trader. This is often overlooked as a key element for a trader, but I believe it is important because a journal helps you be aware of potential performance growth components as well as keeping you aware of the things that are hindering performance.

Journaling can be a powerful tool for personal growth and self-improvement. One way to use journaling as a feedback loop is to regularly reflect on your thoughts, feelings, and behaviors, and then make adjustments based on what you learn. This process, known as Kaizen in Japanese culture, is a continuous improvement method that focuses on small, incremental changes over time.

Getting feedback is important for several reasons. Firstly, it allows you to identify patterns in your behavior and thought process that you may not have been aware of. This can help you to understand yourself better and to make more informed decisions. Secondly, feedback can help you to identify areas where you need to improve and set goals for yourself. It can also help you to measure your progress over time.

Kaizen is a way of life. It is a mindset that is deeply ingrained in Japanese culture and business. This philosophy is based on the belief that small, consistent improvements lead to big changes over time. This approach is used in many Japanese companies, and it is also used in personal development. By regularly reflecting on your thoughts and actions, you can make small improvements that will lead to big changes in the long run.

Using journaling as a feedback loop can be a powerful tool for personal growth and self-improvement. Regularly reflecting on your thoughts, feelings, and behaviors, and making small adjustments based on what you learn, can help you to understand yourself better and make more informed decisions.

Journaling will also increase awareness of your strengths and weaknesses.

You do not know what you do not know, and if you do not write it down in a journal, you will not know.

Maintaining a daily trading journal will help you with the following:

1. Measuring your performance
2. Maximizing learning by growing your brain
3. Improving discipline
4. Keeping track of your execution (that you are trading the entries correctly)
5. Maintaining awareness of your risk
6. Being aware of your emotional thoughts and actions

Measuring performance can be done using a spreadsheet, your brokerage statement, or even a $1 notebook you get at the Dollar Store. I personally use a combination approach of multiple tracking methods.

I have a notebook that I write in each day before the trading session, and I write down my plans and risk management and intentions for the day. This helps me manage my emotions and my actions, so that I do not make any bad decisions in the trading day. A bad decision is not a losing trade. A bad decision is when I violate my rules or take action based on emotions.

I also follow up here with how the previous day went and how I felt about that day.

Intentional Journaling to Improve Brain Function

Dr. Caroline Leaf, a neuroscientist with over 30 years of research and study on the brain, wrote a book called *Cleaning Up Your Mental Mess*,[10] in which she discusses a process called a "neuro cycle," which helps you create neuro pathways to improve brain performance and create better thinking patterns.

I have adopted this five-step process for my trading, and it has dramatically improved my performance and discipline as a trader. When I adopted this method, I saw immediate improvement by taking the time to work on my brain and mindset rather than just focus on trading.

Here is how the neuro cycle works.

1. **Awareness:** Think of a problem or thought pattern that you would like to change.
2. **Reflect:** Continue to think about this for a little while.
3. **Write:** Write down everything you think about the problem or thought pattern.

4. Reassess: Think about everything you thought about and wrote down.
5. Action: Write down an action plan—what you are going to do every time this problem or thought pattern comes up.

Continue to do this each day with a problem until you destroy it. Make using the neuro cycle in your life a pattern that will help you build a healthy thought life and good habits.

Here is how I have used this to help me become a better trader.

I was aware that I had a difficult time with discipline and following my risk management rules as closely as possible.

Then, using the five steps of neuro cycle awareness (reflect, write, reassess, and action), I came up with the strategy of taking a break after every losing trade. This helps keep me from jumping back into a trade, which is sometimes called "revenge trading." Revenge trading, as discussed in Chapter 1, is trying to get back the money you lost by immediately jumping right back into the market and sometimes making larger trades because you are so focused on making your money back right away.

Using Online Brokerage and Charting Patterns to Track Results

I use my online brokerage statements to track my individual trades. There are also third-party tracking platforms like Trader Vue or EdgeWonk that show more data. I also have created a spreadsheet where I manually enter each trade. Whatever method you decide to use, it is important to review your trading each week so that you can constantly improve.

It is important for you to work on your trading process because the more you work on your process, the better your trading will be.

It is so important to focus on process rather than on profit and loss because if you focus on profit and loss, you are not focusing on the act of trading. When the majority of your energy is focused on your profits, it is easier to get emotional and make emotional trading decisions rather than focusing on your process.

I review my trades every day. I check for the following:

- Trade entry point
- Trade management
- Trade exit
- Risk management

Doing this helps me truly get a deeper understanding of how I am trading and why I enter a trade. I add these into my spreadsheet. I also add notes that I can review later so that I will not forget what I learned during the trading process. It is important to always be working on yourself, so that you become a better and better trader.

I also do a weekly review process. I review my weekly performance as a whole, and one of my goals is to be profitable each week, although I might not always succeed. When I review my weekly performance, I notice whether I am profitable and whether I gave back those profits, resulting in a losing week.

I have learned how to protect profits by trading safely. Once I have a profit, I lock it in for the week. I protect profits by trading less frequently, trading only my favorite setups and only taking one trade at a time. Once I have made money, I do not want to let that money get away from me.

Trading is not just about making money but also about keeping the money you have already made.

I learned by doing weekly performance reviews that I had a habit of giving up my profits with undisciplined trading, and many times a weekly profit would disappear because I was greedy and trying to make that weekly profit much more than what I should have.

Once I implemented the weekly review, I was a much better trader long term.

The next part of the review process is to look at a monthly review of my trading. Building on my weekly goal, my goal is to be profitable each month. By reviewing monthly performance, I have learned how to get ahead in the month quickly and then hold on to my profit.

Additionally, these monthly reviews help me see patterns in my trading to help find problems and where I can see what I am doing well and make that work even better.

This is one reason why continuous journaling and review is important because if you start to slip, you will find out right away and be able to respond to the slide.

Keeping a consistent trading journal will help you consistently improve over time, and that is all we can ask for as traders because we know if we are always getting better, we will always be making more money.

Improving Mindset through Study and Education

One of the best investments you can make is an investment in yourself. If you are a trader, there is never a point when you have "made it"; you can always improve.

If you are not learning, you are not growing. If you're not growing, you're declining, and if you start to lose your edge, you will not be a successful trader.

To grow as a trader it is important to love learning.

I love to learn. It keeps me sharp and keeps my mind and spirit engaged. I do not have to always be learning about trading;

I love to read biographies and history. I like to learn about business and entrepreneurship.

I spend time learning to become a better trader. I signed up for courses and masterminds. I learn from trading mentors and business mentors; I also have spiritual mentors. I have a lot to give because I am always feeding and learning.

If you can develop this love for learning, it can have a huge impact on your trading and overall happiness in life.

If you are successful and have a system that works, then you do not necessarily have to learn a new system or even continue to take additional trading education. But it is important to spend your time learning and growing.

Build learning and education into your daily schedule so you can learn new things each day.

One other important component of education is being prepared for each trading day and each trading week.

Preparation is a crucial step in achieving success in any endeavor, and trading is no exception. Taking the time to prepare before each trading day can help you make better-informed decisions, stay updated on market news and events, and set yourself up for success.

One of the key benefits of preparation is that it allows you to identify patterns and make better decisions in the future. Reviewing past trades and performance can help you understand your strengths and weaknesses as a trader, and make adjustments accordingly.

Being aware of current events and staying updated on market news and events is also important. This can help you make more informed decisions about what to trade and when.

Preparation also helps to get you in the right mindset for trading. Trading can be stressful, so it's important to take the time to mentally prepare for the day ahead.

Preparation is a key step in achieving success as a trader. It allows you to make better decisions, stay updated on market news and events, and get in the right mindset for the day ahead. Make sure to take the time to prepare each day before you start trading.

Summary

In order to be successful in trading, it is essential to develop a strong mindset. This chapter delves into various elements that contribute to building such a mindset.

Firstly, committing to the process is crucial. In order to achieve success, one must be willing to put in the time and effort required. Additionally, it is important to have a long-term perspective and not to get discouraged by short-term setbacks.

Believing in eventual success is another key component. A positive attitude and belief in oneself can go a long way in achieving success in trading.

Taking responsibility for one's trading is also vital. It is important to take ownership of one's actions and not blame outside factors for losses.

Developing a mindset of integrity is equally important. Honesty and transparency in trading practices are crucial for building trust and maintaining a good reputation.

Controlling what one can and releasing the rest is a necessary mindset. Focusing on what can be controlled, rather than wasting energy on things that cannot be controlled, is essential for success.

Good habits, such as discipline, patience, and persistence, also play a crucial role in becoming a successful trader. Additionally, planning for failure is important, as it helps to have a plan in place in case things do not go as planned.

Keeping a trading journal is an important tool for tracking progress and learning from past mistakes. Furthermore, self-education and constant learning are an ongoing process in becoming a successful trader.

In conclusion, this chapter highlights the various elements that contribute to developing a strong trading mindset. By committing to the process, believing in eventual success, taking responsibility, maintaining integrity, controlling what one can, developing good habits, planning for failure, keeping a trading journal, and constantly learning, one can lay the foundation for a successful trading career.

Notes

1. https://www.ncbi.nlm.nih.gov/pmc/articles/PMC4662388/#:~:text=Throughout%20his%20book%2C%20Gladwell%20repeatedly,at%20least%2010%20000%20hours.

2. https://info.tradingstrategyguides.com/prop-firm-details 1636481181888.

3. https://hbswk.hbs.edu/item/what-the-stockdale-paradox-tells-us-about-crisis-leadership.

4. https://blog.hubspot.com/sales/jim-rohn-quotes.

5. https://podcast.tradingstrategyguides.com/destroy-the-biggest-obstacle-to-trading-success-in-one-step-with-casey-stubbs-ep-123/.

6. https://www.orionphilosophy.com/stoic-blog/viktor-frankl-greatest-quotes.

7. https://jamesclear.com/atomic-habits.

8. https://podcast.tradingstrategyguides.com/michael-patak-trading-discipline-foundational-to-success-ep-29/.

9. https://yourtradingcoach.com/trader/improve-your-edge-with-a-mental-reset-ritual/.

10. https://www.amazon.com/Cleaning-Your-Mental-Mess-Scientifically/dp/0801093457.

Chapter 3
How Markets Work: Knowing This Gives You an Edge

This chapter explains how markets work and why markets move the way they do. This will give you a foundation of what is happening behind the scenes. This knowledge will assist you in doing the research you will need in preparing to enter your trading positions.

Factors Responsible for Market Movement

The following list is just a small sample of the different factors that cause markets to move.

1. **Economic data and indicators:** Market moves based on the release of economic data such as GDP, employment, inflation, and others.
2. **Interest rates:** Changes in interest rates set by central banks affect the cost of borrowing, which influences investment

and spending. This increases money supply, which has a dramatic effect on market dynamics.

3. **Global events and news:** Market fluctuations can result from significant global events and news, such as natural disasters, political upheavals, and trade agreements.

4. **Political and geopolitical developments:** Market movements are impacted by political developments within countries and geopolitical relations between nations.

5. **Supply and demand dynamics:** Market prices are determined by the balance between supply and demand for goods and services.

6. **Sentiment and investor behavior:** Market movements can be influenced by the overall sentiment of investors and their collective actions.

7. **Technological advancements:** Technological breakthroughs can disrupt traditional market players and create new opportunities for growth.

8. **Natural disasters and emergencies:** Market fluctuations can occur as a result of natural disasters and emergencies, such as hurricanes, earthquakes, and pandemics.

9. **Central bank policies:** Central banks can influence market movements through their monetary policies, such as setting interest rates or printing money.

10. **Competition and market saturation:** Market movements can be affected by competition within industries and the saturation of particular markets.

11. **Emotions of traders:** Fear and greed are massive factors that cause market movements.

It is challenging to fully understand why markets move, as there are multiple factors at play, some of which may be unknown or unpredictable. Market movements are influenced by a combination of economic, political, social, and psychological factors, as well as by sudden events such as natural disasters or global emergencies.

Additionally, investor sentiment and behavior play a significant role in market movements, and it can be difficult to predict how individual investors or groups of investors will react in any given situation. Therefore, while it is possible to analyze and understand the general influences on market movements, it is impossible to predict with certainty why markets move.

Most traders do not learn about market mechanics in depth; by reading and understanding this chapter you will have an edge. In Chapter 1 I mentioned that one of the biggest obstacles traders face is thinking that they only need to know strategy and thus leave out many other important parts of market dynamics. This is a massive error in thinking and because of this most traders never learn the fundamental reason markets move the way they do.

We see "candles" on charts. We know that prices are going up or down, but we do not understand why or how these prices move. What makes a stock go down in value and how does it work?

I am going to share a concept that I first learned from Lance Beggs in *YTC Price Action Trader*[1] that has been extremely helpful to me. Lance explains that the markets are moved by many factors that we cannot see. Things happen behind the scenes that we are not aware of. In fact, we only see the effect of market movements; we do not see the cause. We have an incomplete picture of the markets, and no matter how much information we have, we will never get the complete picture of why a market is moving.

Beggs uses the allegory of the cave from the Greek philosopher Plato. From Wikipedia:

> Imagine a cave where people have been imprisoned from childhood, but not from birth. These prisoners are chained so that their legs and necks are fixed, forcing them to gaze at the wall in front of them and not to look around at the cave, each other, or themselves. Behind the prisoners is a fire, and between the fire and

the prisoners is a raised walkway with a low wall, behind which people walk carrying objects or puppets "of men and other living things."

The people walk behind the wall so their bodies do not cast shadows for the prisoners to see, but the objects they carry do ("just as puppet showmen have screens in front of them at which they work their puppets").The prisoners cannot see any of what is happening behind them, they are only able to see the shadows cast upon the cave wall in front of them. The sounds of the people talking echo off the walls, and the prisoners believe these sounds come from the shadows.

Socrates suggests that the shadows are reality for the prisoners because they have never seen anything else; they do not realize that what they see are shadows of objects in front of a fire, much less that these objects are inspired by real things outside the cave which they do not see.

The fire, or human-made light, and the puppets, used to make shadows, are done by the artists. Plato, however, indicates that the fire is also the political doctrine that is taught in a nation state. The artists use light and shadows to teach the dominant doctrines of a time and place.

Also, few humans will ever escape the cave. This is not some easy task, and only a true philosopher, with decades of preparation, would be able to leave the cave, up the steep incline. Most humans will live at the bottom of the cave, and a small few will be the major artists that project the shadows with the use of human-made light. . . .[2]

There are too many people and circumstances involved in what moves a market, and when we begin to understand and accept this reality, we become equipped to learn how to profit from the markets.

There are major unknown factors that move markets that we cannot see. Understanding that you can never know everything in the markets will be freeing for you as a trader. This is freeing because if we truly understand that we will never be able to take a perfect trade, we will realize that trading is about probabilities.

We take the best trade we can and use money management techniques to give us a trading edge.

How Emotions Move Markets

I have discovered that having a strong understanding of the markets behind the scenes makes a big difference in how I look at trading and therefore has improved my trading performance.

The market movements we see happening on charts are caused by people buying and selling behind the scenes. All we see are prices going up or going down.

The market will not always make sense because it is being led by emotions. If you want to profit on a consistent basis, you must understand this: humans are led by emotions, and those emotions can cause the price of whatever you are trading to be very volatile—prices moving rapidly in multiple directions without a clearly identifiable reason.

Emotions can be irrational and erratic, which means that often the markets are irrational and erratic. If you do not understand that this is happening in the markets, you can easily get caught up in the market movement, and it can cause a great deal of damage to your account balance.

It is easy for traders to get caught in the emotions of the market. If you start following along, you begin trading purely emotionally and then you are contributing to the chaos of the market. Please be aware of your emotions so that if you get caught up trading emotionally, you will stop before you lose your trading capital.

The two emotions that cause the markets to move are *fear* and *pain*.

1. **Fear** is one of the strongest emotions that a trader must learn to overcome to be successful, and it is one of the most powerful forces involved in causing market prices to move.

Fear can be caused by greed: you are afraid that you will be missing out on the next big trade. This is called FOMO (Fear of Missing Out).

It works like this: you see that the market is making a large price move, and you are on the sidelines. Because you fear missing a massive profit, you enter in a massive trade, which is way bigger than the amount of risk you would normally take. However, because you are being led by fear you did not think much about the risk; you just jumped in with a larger size than you should have.

Being controlled by greed and fear causes many traders to make terrible trading decisions, and that is one of the biggest reasons for the massive market moves we see happening on a daily basis.

2. **Pain** is felt when a trader loses more money than they can mentally handle. This then causes additional irrational decisions because a trader isn't thinking about trading properly but just ending the pain of being in such a massive losing trade.

In the previous example of fear, the trader entered a trade that was too risky. That trader will be in pain. If the market reverses, they now have to deal with a massive loss. That trader might then make additional bad decisions, perhaps refusing to close the trade because they hope that it will turn around.

You might get lucky, and the price might turn around and then you get out of that massive losing trade because you were in too much pain and couldn't bear to take that large of a loss.

This is what I call being rewarded for bad behavior. Sometimes the market will reward a trader for bad behavior. That reinforces the bad behavior, and they will continue to trade in fear and continue to make too-large trades. Eventually, the consequences of negative trading catch up to them, and they have to close the trade with massive losses, or they end up taking a trade so large that they lose their entire trading account.

Day Trading Disaster

I didn't have any day trading experience when I first attempted to day trade in 2008, but I needed money. Earlier in this book I said needing money is a dangerous place to begin learning to trade because you have other financial problems that you need to learn to solve. Learning to trade is an important financial problem that you can learn to solve. If you believe it will be a way to get you out of your situation, you are mistaken.

However, I did not understand that truth at that early point in my trading career.

I started with a small $50 account using a strategy and style of trading that I learned from my first mentor, Michael Storm.

The strategy was excellent, and I was having a lot of early success. The problem is that I didn't understand trading emotions and how that moved markets and how my own trading emotions would motivate me to make trades.

This $50 kept growing despite my inexperience. I kept taking bigger risks and making more money. In a short period of time I had grown this $50 account to over $3,500!

I believed that I had made it—at this point I was making over $100 a day, and I truly believed that I had figured it out.

Can you guess what happened next?

I was afraid of missing a big move, and I got greedy. I increased the size on a trade, and then that trade started to move against me. Then the pain set in, and I couldn't close the trade because it was too painful. I never did have the courage to close the trade. The only way I got out was because of a margin call and that meant that the broker closes the trade because I didn't have any money left.

I was devastated. I worked hard for three months to build that balance up. Every single day slugging it out in the markets spending my time and energy to grow my account to over $3,500. I went from the emotion of invincibility to despair. I was devastated.

The aftereffects of that event were so harmful to me as a trader that I went on a massive downturn, a losing spiral where I continued to have losing week after losing week for six months after this event.

It was such a traumatic event that it created many psychological blocks in my mind that I had to work hard to free myself from.

That traumatic event was also my anchor for future success. Because even though it was devastating to me, I never forgot how I made that $3,500, and I always believed that if I did it once, I could do it again. That kept me going, always pushing forward. I also knew that the massive loss was because of my own reckless trading and did not have anything to do with the markets.

Despite the hard times, that memory of making that money allowed me to never quit.

My friend and trading mentor Kevin Pyne from TradingBuddySystem.com, whom I interviewed on the *How to Trade It* podcast, taught me a great way to handle my emotions. He created a chart called the emotion tracker.[3]

Kevin explains that emotions can swing wildly, and we must be aware of them in our trading. He outlines these in Figure 3.1.

Each day before you trade, during trading, and after you trade you can review this chart and write down the words that describe what you are feeling. Then make sure you are not allowing these emotions to carry into your trades for that day. If you trade with your emotions, you will be erratic and you will be up and down in your trading, eventually causing failure.

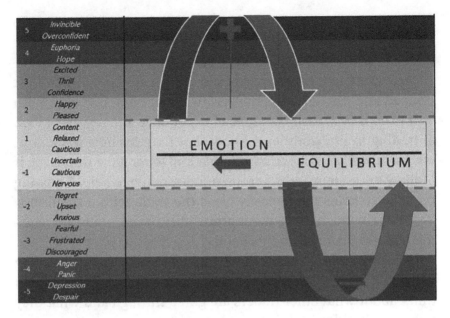

Figure 3.1 Emotions to Be Aware Of
SOURCE: TradingBuddySystem.com.

The entire purpose of this is to help you understand that the market is moved by emotion and crowd mentality and if you understand this and you do not trade like the rest of the market, you will have a massive edge in your trading.

Trapped Traders

One way to get an edge in trading is to think about what other traders are experiencing in the market. As we understand fear, greed, euphoria, and pain, we know that these are the real market movers. A sudden reversal at a key level can mean that there are *trapped traders*.

Trapped traders are traders who get into a trade because they think the market is breaking out, but instead of a breakout the market reverses and traps traders in a losing position. How do we know that this exists? I know because this has been me many times! I have been trapped in the past and will be trapped again.

I have enough experience in the markets to know when I get trapped and can close the trade with no emotion involved. I am able to do this so easily because of experience and because I look at trading in probabilities. I know that I am losing a trade now, but I will easily come back from that and win on the next trade if I follow my system and do proper money management. Knowing probability helps me to easily close the trade with a small loss. We will talk much more about probability in the money management section later on in this book.

Now we cannot know who is trapped or who is experiencing greed, but it has always been helpful to me to look at charts and think about what other traders are going through and what they might be thinking or doing (see Figure 3.2).

When we are calm and follow good money management and trade management, we will always come out ahead because we know that most traders are not able to do that. Most traders are ruled by emotions, which always ends with trading failure.

But not you! Because you have read this book and are working on your market mindset, you will be ready each day to approach the markets with level-headed trading tactics.

Figure 3.2   Traders Enter on a Breakout but Get Trapped
SOURCE: Casey Stubbs.

Markets Are Moved by Supply and Demand

Supply and demand is a natural law that is always true in nature. This law is what causes prices to move in the markets. If we understand how this works, it will enable us to get a better grasp on market movement, making us better and more accurate traders.

Specifically, "supply and demand" refers to the amount of goods and services available for people to buy, compared to the amount of goods and services people want to buy. If less of a product than the public wants is produced, the law of supply and demand says that more can be charged for the product. In other words, *supply* is the amount that is available. *Demand* is the desire for the product or service and the amount that people are willing to pay for it.

We see supply and demand happen all the time in our economy. In the documentary *The World According to Jeff Goldblum*, Episode 1: Sneakers,[4] Jeff goes to Sneaker Con, a massive market for sneaker fanatics.

During the episode he shows what a massive demand can do to raise sneaker prices. A normal pair of shoes averages less than $100 a pair, but at this convention there are shoes that have massive resale value because of supply and demand—certain shoes are in limited supply combined with people who have money and are willing to pay. At the 2022 Sneaker Con there is a pair of Louis Vuitton Nike Air Force One that has an average resale price of $126,500.[5]

Supply and demand has always been the driving factor for price movements. Looking back in time, we can see the famous Dutch Tulip Market Bubble. This story can help us understand how markets work and also give us greater understanding that will help us become better traders.

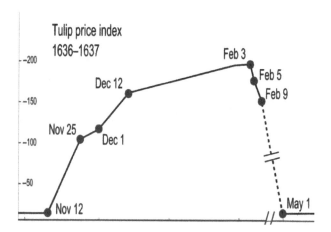

Figure 3.3 When Demand Dries Up, Price Rapidly Falls
SOURCE: https://www.history.com/news/tulip-mania-financial-crash-holland.

In Holland in 1634 the Dutch discovered that tulips could grow 10 times faster from a bulb than from a seed, creating extremely high demand for bulbs. The price started to go up, and as the price went up people had a greater desire to get these bulbs. Why was the demand so high? Because of fear and greed, people wanted to make money, and they would buy the bulbs. Their fear of missing out on the potential profit created massive demand.[6]

Then, when prices started to stall, people again became afraid that prices were going to drop. Then they couldn't sell fast enough,, and the demand dropped and the price dropped much faster than it had risen (see Figure 3.3).

Identify Supply and Demand on Charts

Supply and demand can be seen on trading charts, which can be used to help traders find entries by utilizing this powerful law of nature. The first way to identify supply and demand is to use *price levels*.

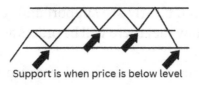

Support is when price is below level

Figure 3.4 The Arrows Show Support Levels
SOURCE: Casey Stubbs.

The levels are called "support" and "resistance." They are created when price changes direction. Support happens when the price has been moving lower, then stops going down, reverses, and begins to climb. The area where price changed direction is a support level (see Figure 3.4).

Resistance occurs where supply and demand have driven the price above the current price. If price is moving up and then stops and changes direction, the area where price reverses is called resistance (see Figure 3.5).

These levels are very important because they show you at what price the supply and demand are located. This causes price to react at those levels because traders create supply and demand at those levels.

Traders all over the world can see these levels displayed on their charts. They will put buy and sell orders based on these levels. The buy and sell orders are what create the supply and demand.

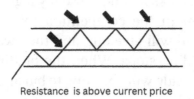

Resistance is above current price

Figure 3.5 The Arrows Show Resistance Points
SOURCE: Casey Stubbs.

Anytime we can clearly see support and resistance levels on our charts, we know that there will be orders accumulating when those levels occur.

This is important to understand because it helps us know when to get into the market ahead of time. Being aware of these levels will help you know when to enter and exit a trade.

Stock Markets Have the Same Behavior as Traditional Markets

Have you ever been to a crowded Saturday morning market where people are waiting in line to get some of the most important items? Maybe you can remember going to an auction and bidding on that item you had to have.

I remember the first time I went to an auction. They had a 2000 Dodge Neon for $500 starting bid. I thought, are you kidding me, this car would cost at least $3,000!

I got excited and started to bid right away because I wanted to get this car so cheap. I think that might have been a bit of greed to get me started because I wanted the deal. Next thing I know I am in a bidding war with someone, and the price is moving up fast. I stopped caring about the deal, and I just wanted the car because this other bidder was trying to take my car away from me!

Again more emotions—the emotion of wanting to win, the competitive spirit kicks in, and I lose my logic.

At some point in the competition for winning the prize, someone's bankroll will give out, and they won't pay the price, and then the bidding stops. When the bidding slows down or stops, the winning side will continue to bid and drive the price to the next area of orders.

Have you ever been in a situation like that?

What about when you are trading? Trading prices in a market move just like in an auction: people are bidding, and buyers and sellers are putting in bids and offers to take control of the price. These pricing battles often occur around areas of support and resistance because of supply and demand. Many traders believe that this area is too expensive, and prices go down. Many others believe it is cheap, and prices will go up.

Eventually one side will lose the bidding, and price will break away from the area and move in a clear direction. Just like when I was buying the Neon, buyers or sellers will run out of capital or conviction and give up, and the price will move in one clear direction.

Use the Magnet for Your Benefit

Price can be compared to a magnet. A magnet works by producing a magnetic field. This magnetic field is generated by the movement of electrons in the magnet, creating north and south poles. When a magnetic field is applied to a ferromagnetic material, the electrons align in the same direction, resulting in the material becoming magnetized. This magnetic field can then attract or repel other magnets or magnetic materials. The strength of the magnetic field depends on the type of material and the arrangements of the electrons. Something similar happens in markets.

Price is drawn like a magnet to where the buyers and sellers are ready to make trades. What this means is that price is attracted to the prices where the orders are located. To understand this, I'll briefly explain how "stop losses" and "take profits" work.

Definition of Stop Loss

A stop loss is an order to sell your trade for a loss at a point at which you believe you were wrong about the trade. Stop loss means you stop losing money. Using stop losses is something that a successful trader always does.

This keeps your losses small and allows you to continue to trade. If you do not use a stop loss, you can experience catastrophic losses that can end your trading career.

Stop losses are an important concept to understand about how markets move and work. Because stop losses are so important, most traders are using them to limit risk on their trading accounts.

Definition of Take Profit

A take profit is an order that a trader sets to automatically close a position when a certain profit level has been reached. In other words, it's a way to lock in profits when the price of an asset reaches a predetermined level.

Having a take profit order is important in trading because it helps to manage risk. By setting a take profit, a trader can limit their potential losses and ensure they capture a portion of the profits made on a trade.

It also takes the emotion out of the equation, as the trader does not have to manually close the position and can instead focus on other trades. In addition, take profit orders can help traders stick to their trading plan and avoid making impulsive decisions that could negatively impact their profits.

Now that we know what stop loss orders and take profit orders are, we can begin to realize that where those stops and take profits are. There will be a large number of orders at that price level. That is what price is drawn to—the areas where there are a large number of orders.

This is a huge edge for us to understand because we can use the price magnet effect to help us get a probability edge in our trading.

If there is a price battle around a key support or resistance level, all of the buyers and sellers at that level finish trading. Some traders hit their take profit; other traders hit the stop loss. Some traders get fearful and finally close the trade.

Stop Losses and Take Profits Create Massive Order Flow

The location of these stop losses is usually put at supply and demand levels, also known as support and resistance. Because all of these stop losses are set near the same price, most of them trigger at the same point. When this happens, the buyers and sellers slow down trading and volume dries up. Volume is the amount of shares or transactions that are taking place during a specific period of time.

Trading volume and order flow can be called liquidity. These are all different words to describe the same thing: buyers and sellers changing hands. This is important for traders to understand because the market needs a large number of buyers and sellers to push prices to new levels.

At each support or resistance level, there is a battle between buyers and sellers to determine whether price is going to continue to go up or reverse. This battle is decided by the number of buyers or sellers. When the battle for a level is decided and the liquidity or order flow is dried up, the price will move to the next level, looking for where there is a large block of buyers and sellers.

Price will move like a magnet to the next level. Nature abhors a vacuum: when there are no orders, price gets sucked right to the area on the charts where there are orders stacked. Then price will continue in that process all over again, and that is how the markets work. This happens many times a day in many markets all over the world, and we as traders know this and wait for the process to happen; then we take advantage of it to trade for profit.

Summary

This chapter explores the complex and dynamic world of markets and how they function. Understanding the factors that drive market movements is crucial for investors, traders, and market participants.

- **Factors Responsible for Market Movement:** Many factors can impact the movement of markets, including economic indicators, geopolitical events, and changes in supply and demand. It is important to stay informed about these factors and how they can influence market trends.
- **How Emotions Move Markets:** Emotions play a significant role in market movements, with fear and greed often driving market behavior. Traders must be mindful of their emotions and strive to make rational, data-driven decisions.
- **How Supply and Demand Works:** The movement of prices in markets is driven by the balance between supply and demand. When demand is high and supply is low, prices tend to rise. Conversely, when demand is low and supply is high, prices tend to fall.
- **Stock Markets Are the Same as Traditional Markets:** The principles of supply and demand are the same in stock markets as they are in traditional markets, such as commodities or real estate. In both cases, price moves like a magnet toward supply and demand levels.

Markets are complex systems that are influenced by a variety of factors, including economic indicators, emotions, and supply and demand. To succeed in the markets, it is important to understand these factors and how they impact market behavior. By staying informed and making data-driven decisions, traders can navigate the markets with confidence and achieve their investment goals.

Notes

1. https://yourtradingcoach.com/ytc-price-action-trader/.
2. https://en.wikipedia.org/wiki/Allegory_of_the_cave.
3. https://podcast.tradingstrategyguides.com/kevin-pyne-emotional-equilibrium/.
4. https://www.imdb.com/title/tt10890288.
5. https://www.complex.com/sneakers/most-expensive-sneakers/louis-vuitton-nike-air-force-1-sothebys.
6. https://www.investopedia.com/terms/d/dutch_tulip_bulb_market_bubble.asp.

Part II

Technical Trading of the Market

N ow we get into the technical charting part of the book, which is the foundation for understanding how we enter and exit trades.

Market analysis is also called technical analysis, and this is one of the foundational skills that a trader must understand to become a master trader. What you learn in this chapter is going to give you exactly what you need to become a full-time trader or to make a solid side revenue from trading the markets.

However, I must make a disclaimer: traders need to understand that technical analysis is not a holy grail or a way to win all your trades. Market analysis, however, is a tool that can give you an edge that will catapult you to success. It is one piece of the puzzle that must be learned along the way.

We are going to tackle market and technical analysis the same way and will approach trading as a whole one step at a time.

Here are the different sections of technical analysis that a trader needs to get their skills up to a level where they will be profitable in the markets:

1. Identifying trends
2. Support and resistance levels
3. Chart patterns
4. Technical indicators

Chapter 4
Trend Trading to Get High-Probability Setups

Trend trading is a popular method of investing in the financial markets, where traders aim to profit from price movements in a particular direction. In this chapter, we explore the various aspects of trend trading and how to effectively identify and trade trends. We begin by discussing the key lessons of trend trading, including:

1. **How to identify a trend:** A trend is a general direction in which the price of an asset is moving. Understanding how to identify trends is crucial for traders, as it allows them to make informed decisions and maximize their profits.
2. **The power of a trend compared to a river:** Trends can be compared to a powerful river that carries traders along with it. The longer and stronger the trend, the more profit potential it offers traders.
3. **Technical aspects of a trend:** We delve into the technical aspects of trends, including the use of trend lines, moving

averages, and momentum indicators. These tools help traders to confirm the presence of a trend and make more informed decisions.

4. **How to use a 10 EMA with a trend:** The 10-day exponential moving average (EMA) is a commonly used indicator for trend trading. In this chapter, we discuss how to use the 10 EMA to confirm a trend and make profitable trades.

5. **Simple trend examples:** Finally, we provide several simple trend examples to illustrate the concepts discussed in this chapter. These examples will help traders to understand how to identify trends, confirm their presence, and make profitable trades.

By the end of this chapter, traders will have a strong understanding of trend trading and the key concepts and tools involved in this approach to investing.

A trending market is when the market moves in one direction for a long period of time. This is the best market to trade, and we show you specific guidelines on how to trade trends.

The specific amount of time for a trend depends on which time frame you are trading. You can find trends and trade them on 1-minute charts or monthly charts. The methodology for trading them will be the same. You will know exactly how to identify and trade trends by the end of this chapter.

A Trend Is a Powerful Force

When a trend is moving in a stock or market, it has a lot of power or force to continue moving in that direction. Remember that a market is a group of people with different emotions and beliefs, all trading together. Everyone in that market is looking at the trend and believes that the price will continue to go up or down.

All of the traders will continue to buy or sell because they believe in the trend. This collective belief is what keeps the trend going strong. However, be warned that a trend can reverse quickly, which is why we always practice risk management. The one time you don't have a solid risk plan in place is the time the market reverses on you.

Because the trend is strong, it takes a great deal of money to reverse it, which is one of the reasons that trends can continue for a long time. To get an understanding of the power of trends in a market, think about a massive river that is pouring millions of gallons of water moving downstream. That river is a massive force that carries everything in it downriver. If you jump into that river and swim upstream as hard as you can, the force of the river overpowers you and carries you away.

This is what can happen if you, as a small trader, try to trade against a trend; you will be carried away by the current. Many traders have been taken out over the years because they attempt to trade against the strong trend. Even if your timing isn't great, just staying with the power of the trend can help win more trades and win bigger trades.

You can jump in and just ride the wave of the markets. Just be careful to make sure you get off the wave before it crashes! Later in the chapter, I will show you how to do this.

One of my early experiences with the power of trends was an educational event I attended at the Traders Expo in New York City. James Chen was a presenter there and was teaching about currency power: how when you connect the strongest currency to the weakest you can find the strongest trends. This was such a cool concept; I was so excited to learn this. I was driving back from the expo with Nathan Tucci, my employee at the time, and we planned during the trip home to build a tool to find the strongest and weakest currencies to help us and other traders find the best trends. We immediately contacted a great programmer named Mark Thomas, and he created the Forex Power indicator. That tool is still available at my website today, and it has helped thousands of traders identify the strongest trends.[1]

The Power of Taking Action

As you read about trends and trading, I want you to take some time each day thinking about applying the things you learn. One important lesson from the story above is that I didn't just go to a trading conference. I took action to change my life. I learned valuable skills, and then I applied them to create something useful. Use the skills you are learning in this book to do something great in your life and in the lives of others.

There were thousands of people at that event, but Nathan and I were the only ones who took action. I see this every day in my business. People want great results, but they don't take action.

When you take action, you put a force in motion and build your own trends by creating momentum in your life. Be an action taker.

Technical Aspects of a Trend

One way to identify uptrends is by looking at the charts and seeing if the trend will make higher highs and lower lows. What this means is that the price of a stock will continue to make new highs on a regular basis. When the price does retrace and go down, it will not make a new low; it makes a higher low. This is the easiest way to identify trends—by looking at the chart and observing if it is making higher highs and higher lows.

Figure 4.1 shows what the market structure of higher highs and higher lows looks like.

Trending markets can go either up or down. In a downtrend, you will see the exact opposite of uptrends. In a downtrend, you

Figure 4.1   Higher Highs and Higher Lows in a Proper Uptrend
SOURCE: TradingStrategyGuides.com.

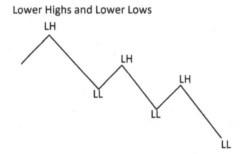

Figure 4.2   Structure of a Downtrend
SOURCE: Casey Stubbs.

will notice that there are lower lows and lower highs. Figure 4.2 shows a strong downtrend—notice the market structure.

One important part of trend trading is noticing how the waves create support and resistance levels as price continues to move, as shown in Figure 4.3.

A great example of a long-term trend is the Standard & Poor's 500, which has been in a strong uptrend for the past 20 years. Figure 4.4 shows that price moves from left to right as it is moving up consistently.

Becomes Resistance on the Way Down

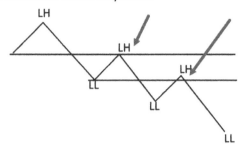

Figure 4.3   Structure of a Downtrend Focusing on Resistance Areas
SOURCE: Casey Stubbs.

Figure 4.4   Long-Term Trend S&P 500
SOURCE: TrendSpider.

The best way to trade the SPX index is to be on the long side of it, which means to be buying. In fact if you bought the S&P 500 at the low of this chart in 2009, it would be at $668. That would be a spectacular trade because the high in 2022 was $4,808. That would give you a profit of $4,140, which is a return of 619%—that would be a great trade!

The main point I want you to take away is that a trader can find a massive edge by trading with the trend and not fighting it. Of course, you *can* trade countertrend, and I know many traders who are successful doing so, but the point I am making is that you can get an edge by trading with the trend, and I always try to take advantage of every advantage I can get in the markets, because in the long term that increases my probability.

Figure 4.4 shows that there were a few trades that could have been made countertrend against the S&P 500. There are, however, two things that stand out against trading against the trend:

1. The countertrend moves were much smaller, which means your profits on the trade are smaller and it will be harder to capture the move.
2. There are fewer trades to be had, which will lower your profits in trading that move.

Overall, trading with the trend provides great benefits for these reasons.

Using the 10 EMA to Identify a Trend

I trade with the trend by applying an indicator on my chart. The indicator that I like to use is the 10 EMA (exponential moving average). A moving average takes the 10 previous candles (a "candle," or candlestick, is a type of price chart used in technical analysis to display the high, low, open, and closing prices of a security for a specific period of time) and gives you the average price between the previous 10 periods. The EMA gives a stronger preference to the most recent candles.

To identify the trend, I apply this to a weekly chart, and if the price is above the 10 EMA on a weekly time frame, that indicates that we are in an uptrend.

Definition of "Time Frame"

A time frame is a period of time that you measure price on a chart. If you select the weekly time frame on your chart, it will display price data in that candle for 1 week. If you select 5 minutes on your chart, it will display 5 minutes of price data on your chart. The common time frames that traders use are: yearly, quarterly, monthly, weekly, daily, 4 hr, 1 hr, 15 min, 5 min, and 1 min.

The longer the time frame you are looking at, the more data is contained inside of that candle, therefore longer time frames are usually much stronger and give better signals. The drawback to longer time frames is that trades are less frequent, and you must use larger stop losses when entering trades. I prefer to use a combination of long and short time frames when placing my trades.

I use the weekly price because a weekly chart gives an entire week of price data on the candle, and that gives a longer view. If you look at the chart on a longer view, that means that you get more data and there is a stronger trend versus if you applied it to a daily chart, which has a shorter view.

A price above a 10 EMA on a weekly chart is much stronger than a price above the 10 EMA on a daily chart. Figure 4.5 shows 10 EMA on a weekly chart.

The uptrend shown in Figure 4.5 is getting ready to start again, and there is a buy signal because the weekly trend just crossed above the 10 EMA.

That is very simple: if the price is above the 10 EMA and we are making higher highs and lower lows, we are in a downtrend. If the price is below 10 EMA and we are making lower lows, we are in a downtrend.

Figure 4.5 SPY Trend Continuation Trade Setup
SOURCE: TrendSpider.

I will always stick with the current trend to find the best trades.

Trend Line Breaks

One great way to trade trends is to try to find a new trend and trade that. I do this by drawing something called a *trend line*. You draw a diagonal line on the top of the candles of a trend moving up or down (see Figure 4.6).

If you have patience to wait for trend line breaks on a daily chart, that will consistently yield high probability setups.

Trend lines can be traded when there is a long-term trend and price changes indicating a new trend taking place.

There are two basic ways that I trade a trend.

1. The first method is that you enter the trade as soon as price closes on the other side of the trend line.
2. The second method is that you wait until price breaks the trend line and then comes back to test a new support level. This method requires more patience for the trader. However, it helps to eliminate getting faked out on a fake break because the new trend is more established.

Figure 4.6   Trend Line Breaks Are a Type of Resistance Break and Can Be Effective Entry Points
SOURCE: TrendSpider.

How to Trade with the Trend

I am going to share a very simple trend trading strategy that you can backtest for yourself to determine if it will work or not. By "backtest" I mean to go back and look at all the times this particular trade setup happened in the past and then chart it as if you were trading it to determine if the trade is successful or not.

I recommend doing this on any strategy for a minimum of 100 trades before trading it with live money. That might seem extreme to you, because it will take a lot of time to do this, but if you are willing to do the things that others are not willing to do, that by itself will give you an edge. Remember, we are trading against a massive number of people, and if we do the extra work when others do not, it will practically guarantee our success in the markets.

The Simple Trend Trading Strategy

I am going to lay out this strategy in the following clear steps.

1. Find a chart with a clear trend of higher highs or lower lows.
2. Apply a 10 EMA to the chart on a weekly time frame.
3. When price on the trend dips below the 10 EMA and then goes back above, that is a buy signal.
4. Place your stop loss below the candle.
5. Place your take profit so that you will make a minimum of double your risk. For example, if you risk $100 on the trade, you want to make a minimum of $200.

> There will be more on risk management later on in this book because this is an extremely important part of trading that you will need to master if you expect to become a successful trader.

Figure 4.7 shows examples of some trades using this trend strategy.

The arrows in Figure 4.7 are places where the trend continues and would be high-probability places to enter into the trade.

Figure 4.7 shows the consolidation phase before a move. The consolidation phase means that price is going sideways and ranging before the trend continues.

A *ranging market* is a market condition in which the price of an asset moves within a specific range, without any clear trend or direction. It is characterized by a lack of volatility and a repetitive pattern of price movement, often remaining within a well-defined support and resistance level. In this type of market, the price may

Figure 4.7   Areas to Enter Trend Trades
SOURCE: TrendSpider.

oscillate between these levels, creating a series of higher highs and lower lows, but it does not break out in either direction. In a ranging market, traders may use technical analysis techniques to identify key levels and make decisions on whether to buy or sell an asset.

This happens often in trends. It is a good idea to wait until the consolidation phase is over before getting into the trade. Learning to spot these consolidations is a great way to find a trade before it takes off. It is good to find consolidation patterns (see Figure 4.8).

One point I want to add: to make a trend trade even stronger, have a clear support or resistance level to trade off of (see Figure 4.9). When price bounces off of support or resistance, this is an additional confirmation in your trading because as I explained earlier in the book, traders will stack orders on those levels, and in a trend there is a large supply of buy orders at those levels that can push the prices higher.

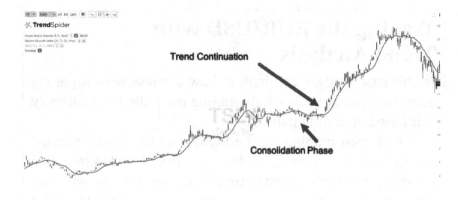

Figure 4.8 Ranging or Consolidating Market before Trend Continues
SOURCE: TrendSpider.

Figure 4.9 Trend Trade off of Resistance Level
SOURCE: TrendSpider.

Trading the EUR/USD with Trend Analysis

In this case study, I will look at how I was able to triple my account value by successfully trading the EUR/USD currency pair based on trend analysis.

I had been monitoring the EUR/USD for several months and noticed that it was in a clear downtrend. I identified this trend using a combination of trend lines and moving averages, including the 10-day exponential moving average (10 EMA). I also used support and resistance levels to determine key areas where buying or selling pressure was likely to enter the market.

Based on my analysis, I decided to enter a sell trade on the EUR/USD. I placed my trade at the market price when the currency pair reached a key resistance level and the 10 EMA indicated a downtrend.

The trade was a success, and the EUR/USD continued to move lower over the next few weeks. I was able to enter the trend again at two additional points, using the 10 EMA and support and resistance levels as my guide. By the end of the trade, I had successfully tripled the value of my account.

This case study highlights the power of trend analysis in currency trading. By identifying a clear downtrend in the EUR/USD, I was able to enter the market at multiple points and capitalize on the trend for a significant profit. It also highlights the importance of using a combination of technical tools, such as trend lines, moving averages, and support and resistance levels, to confirm and enhance my analysis.

Summary

Trend trading is a great strategy to use, and I highly recommend that beginning traders start out using that strategy to enter into the markets.

- Identifying a Trend
  - A trend refers to the direction of price movement over a period of time.
  - Trends can be identified through trend lines, moving averages, and momentum indicators.
  - An uptrend is characterized by consistently higher prices, while a downtrend is characterized by consistently lower prices.
- The Power of a Trend Compared to a River
  - A trend in the market can be compared to a river, with the current (trend) carrying prices in a specific direction.
  - The strength of a trend is determined by the strength of buying or selling pressure.
  - Traders should aim to swim with the current (trend) to maximize profits and minimize risk.
- Technical Aspects of a Trend
  - The technical aspects of a trend include support and resistance levels, chart patterns, and indicators.
  - Support levels indicate where buying pressure is likely to enter and push prices higher in a trend.
  - Resistance levels indicate where selling pressure is likely to enter and push prices lower in a trend.
- Using a 10 EMA with a Trend
  - The 10-day exponential moving average (10 EMA) is a popular trend-following indicator.

- The 10 EMA is calculated by taking the average of the past 10 days of closing prices and plotting it on the price chart.
- The 10 EMA acts as a dynamic support or resistance level and can be used to identify the direction of the trend.
- Simple Trend Examples
  - Trends can be seen in overall markets, such as a bull market in stocks or a bear market in commodities.
  - Trends can also be seen in individual securities, such as a stock in an uptrend or a currency in a downtrend.
  - It is important to regularly monitor and adjust trading strategies as trends can change over time.

Note

1. https://tradingstrategyguides.com/forex-power-indicator/.

Chapter 5

Support and Resistance Level Trading Strategy

Welcome to this chapter on trading with support and resistance. In the world of trading, understanding key price levels can be a valuable tool for maximizing profits and minimizing risks. That's where support and resistance come in. Support and resistance levels are critical elements in technical analysis and provide traders with a clear and objective approach to the market.

In this chapter, you will learn about the strength of support and resistance levels, the difference between horizontal and sloping levels, how to use support and resistance as a system, and the power of level trading. You will also discover the importance of consolidation in levels and how to trade using support and resistance levels.

Whether you are a beginner or an experienced trader, this chapter will provide valuable insights into how to use support and resistance levels in your trading strategy. So, buckle up and get ready to dive into the world of support and resistance.

Chapter 3 briefly explained how support and resistance work in the market as this strategy is one of the key fundamental aspects of trading. This chapter is going to explain how to trade with support and resistance.

A support level is where price has stopped previously and reversed below current price. Resistance is where price has stopped previously and reversed above the current price. Support acts as a floor, and resistance acts as a ceiling, and these are areas where we will typically see traders place trades.

This book is set up to build skills, one on top of another, to give you a complete set of tools, which you can use to become a successful trader. Support and resistance is one tool that you will want to get skilled at to determine how to identify these levels.

Strength of Levels

If you view your charts at different time frames, you will see different levels. For example, if you look at a 15-minute chart and then change the time frame to weekly, you will no longer see the levels that you saw on the 15-minute time frame. This is because when you go to a weekly chart you are zooming out and cannot see the same level of detail. When you zoom back in, you will be able to see those levels again.

The longer the time frame you are looking at, the stronger the level is, and the more likely it is that you will see prices react at that specific level. Since you are zooming out to get a longer time frame, on a weekly chart the levels you see will be much bigger since you are able to see them so far away. That means that they are important levels that other traders will be able to see as well.

Because I know that longer time frame levels are stronger, I want to always be aware of where they are located, even when I am zooming in. To keep track of strong levels when zooming in,

Figure 5.1   Support and Resistance Levels—Begin Practicing Drawing Them
SOURCE: TrendSpider.

use horizontal levels and diagonal levels. Both types of levels can and should be used in your analysis of the trend.

Horizontal Levels

Horizontal levels run from side to side—you draw resistance levels on the top of the candles and the support levels on the bottom of the candles. Figure 5.1 shows horizontal support and resistance levels.

Sloping Levels

Diagonal levels are drawn from the tops and bottoms of the candles using a sloping line moving up or down. Figure 5.2 shows sloping levels.

Notice in Figure 5.2 the channel that is in place. Many traders do well using the channel trading strategy by buying and selling as the price bounces off the channel at this good location for trading.

Figure 5.2   This Is a Trend—Channel Support Is at the Bottom and Resistance at the Top of the Channel
SOURCE: TrendSpider.

Level Analysis System

I have a specific system that I use every day when trading the markets to identify the most important levels.

First, I look at the chart on a weekly level. I identify two support levels above current price and two resistance levels above current price. I do this by drawing a horizontal line using my charting software. I look for horizontal levels as well as diagonal levels.

The software I currently use is called TrendSpider. It has a large variety of markets I can chart with it, as well as with a large variety of tools I can choose from.

Next, I zoom in to daily charts and draw all of the levels on the daily time frame.

If I am going to be day trading, I will zoom in one more time and mark all of the levels in a 15-minute time frame as well. If I am not day trading, I will stop at the daily levels.

Since I have weekly levels, daily levels, and also 15-minute time frame levels, I will color-code each type of level so that I can see which ones are more important. (The weekly levels are the most important since they are the largest levels.)

Now that I have the levels all marked on my charts, it is time to begin to plan my trades.

I wait for price to touch the level, and I wait to see if we get a reversal on the chart. I use candlestick patterns to identify if a reversal is happening. In Chapter 6, we dive into the details of how to use reversal patterns to enter trades.

I also use a 10 EMA (see Chapter 4) on the time frame I am trading to wait until price breaks above or below the 10 EMA after bouncing off a level.

Figure 5.3 Bitcoin Is Breaking a Support Level, Which Indicates More Selling Ahead
SOURCE: TrendSpider.

Figure 5.4   Buy on a Bounce of Support as Shown in the Image
SOURCE: TrendSpider.

If I get a price pattern with a break above the EMA, I will take a buy trade with a stop loss below that level.

Figures 5.3 and 5.4 show two example trades. Figure 5.3 shows a downtrend and a weekly break below an important level along with a close below the 10 EMA in bitcoin.

The Power of Level Trading

This section discusses several key advantages of using levels. Of course, trading with levels does not always work, because sometimes you are expecting a bounce but the momentum is so strong approaching a level that it busts right through and keeps on going.

This is why I always wait for the bounce to happen before I take a trade. As I say many times in this book, there is no such thing as a perfect trade. This is why we stay consistent with the execution of our strategy and always use proper risk management.

Using Levels to Improve Trading

This is an example of how I have been able to multiply my trading account many times over. How did I do it? The key to my success was consistency with weekly levels.

I had been trading for several years and was always on the lookout for ways to improve my performance. I realized that one of the biggest challenges I faced was staying disciplined and sticking to my strategy. That's when I discovered the importance of weekly levels in my trading.

I started using weekly support and resistance levels as a guide for my trades. I made it a habit to review these levels every week and adjust my trading plan accordingly. This helped me stay focused and consistent with my trades. I found that by using weekly levels, I was able to identify key areas where the price was likely to change direction, giving me a significant edge in my trades.

One of the keys to my success was my ability to stick to my strategy and remain consistent, even when faced with losses. I understood that the market can be unpredictable, and I was prepared for that. Instead of making impulsive decisions based on emotions, I relied on my weekly levels and stuck to my plan.

The results of my consistent approach speak for themselves. Over time, I was able to multiply my trading account many times over and become a successful trader. I attributed my success to the power of consistency and the use of weekly levels in my trading strategy.

One of the biggest advantages to using levels is the ability to have smaller stop losses, which will exponentially increase your gains over time. This will be explained in detail in the money management section. It is a mathematical factor of trading that says if you keep your losses small and have bigger wins over time, you will have a profitable trading strategy.

It is better to trade near support and resistance levels, because if you trade in the middle of two levels, you may experience larger losses. This is because oftentimes price consolidates around levels and gives you an opportunity to have smaller stops. The consolidation creates a smaller price range, and this is why the stop losses can be smaller.

The best point to place a stop loss is below the level because of the increased probability of winning the trade.

Trading in the middle of a price zone, which means not waiting for price to reach a support and resistance level, is sometimes called no-man's land.

Trading in the middle of a range can cause a trader to have the following issues.

- **Larger loss size in dollar amount**—because a proper place to put a stop loss is above or below a key level, and in the middle of a zone you cannot do this.
- **Higher loss rate**—because if you trade in the middle of a price zone, it is possible for price to be volatile and whip around and take out your stop if you are not placing it below a support or above a resistance level.

Therefore, it will dramatically decrease your win rate to place a trade in the middle of a level. Additionally, you can use a smaller stop loss next to a level.

If you trade near important levels, it will help you lose smaller trades and help you win larger trades.

Figures 5.5 and 5.6 show proper stop loss trading when using support and resistance levels.

Figure 5.5 is an example of a trade that I would not take. The first reason I would not take this trade is because the stop

Figure 5.5   Notice Price Moving with Volatility above in the Range—Avoid Trading There
SOURCE: TrendSpider.

loss is too large and the target does not have enough profit potential—basically the risk isn't worth the reward. If you are going to take a risk, make sure the reward is worth that risk. The target is the top of the resistance area, and in this example I would be risking $3 to make one dollar. This is not enough reward for the trade.

Also, the trade is in the middle of the range—the price could go either direction. It is much better to trade on the support or resistance areas.

Figure 5.6 shows a much better way to take the trade; however, patience is required to wait for the correct setup to occur.

This example is a much better trade because price is on a level, and that increases the probability of winning your trade and getting a larger-sized win. Also, the target now is the same area, but by waiting for a better entry you are now attempting to make $3 and risk $1. This is a much better prospect. You learn

Figure 5.6   Better Location to Take a Trade because of Clear Support and Smaller Stop Loss
SOURCE: TrendSpider.

more about why this is important in the risk management chapter of this book, Chapter 11.

Using levels and stop losses at the correct area will improve your win-loss rate as well as improving your risk-to-reward ratio, so learning how to properly trade these levels is an important skill you must develop as a trader.

Consolidation and Ranging Markets

When price reaches a support or resistance level, there are times when it will bounce right away, and there are other times when the market will range or consolidate. This happens because the market doesn't have a clear winner on either side or there isn't enough volume to push it to one level or the next. This is, however, a great opportunity to see when markets are getting ready to set up.

Figure 5.7   Price Consolidating Near a Resistance Zone before Taking a Massive Drop
SOURCE: TrendSpider.

It is not great to trade during a consolidation because we do not know which way the market is going to trade. It is, rather, a great time to observe the charts and realize that price is getting ready to set up for a move.

When a market is consolidating, traders are accumulating shares, and that is the time when you want to be getting ready to observe the charts to find out where you want to enter. Notice in Figure 5.7 how price trades in a tight range before dropping.

You can see in Figure 5.8 that the price goes sideways and tests the resistance level twice before making the move down. When price moves to the upside, many traders get trapped trying to trade the breakout. Smart traders realize it is a consolidation and take advantage of the move down.

Figure 5.8 Strong Consolidation Phase—Wait for a Breakout to Trade
SOURCE: TrendSpider

How to Trade Using Support and Resistance

Here is a simple step-by-step guideline of how I trade with trends.

1. I identify the support and resistance levels on the chart of any time frame (1 minute, 15 minute, 1 hour, etc.) that I prefer to trade on.
2. I wait for the price to hit the support or resistance level.
3. When price hits the level and then bounces, I will buy on support or short on resistance.
4. I put a stop loss above or below the level.
5. I target the next area of support and resistance as a profit level with a minimum level of risking 1 to 1.

Summary

Support and resistance levels are crucial elements of technical analysis in trading. This chapter covered various aspects of using support and resistance levels, including:

- **Strength of levels:** The strength of a support or resistance level can vary based on factors such as the number of times the price has bounced off the level, the duration of the price staying at the level, and the volume of trading during the price movement.

- **Horizontal levels:** Horizontal support and resistance levels are determined by price levels at which a stock or asset has repeatedly found support or resistance.
- **Sloping levels:** Sloping support and resistance levels are lines drawn at an angle to connect two or more price points.
- **Level system:** Traders use support and resistance levels as a system to identify potential buy and sell points in the market.
- **Power of level trading:** Support and resistance levels can provide traders with a clear and objective approach to trading, helping to identify key levels and assess market sentiment.
- **Using consolidation in levels:** Consolidation can occur when the price of a stock or asset is moving sideways within a range between support and resistance levels. Traders can use this period of consolidation to make informed trading decisions.
- **Trading using support and resistance levels:** Traders can use support and resistance levels to identify potential buy and sell points, as well as to determine their risk management strategy. When the price approaches a support level, traders may consider entering a long position, and when the price approaches a resistance level, traders may consider entering a short position or exiting a long position.

Trading with support and resistance levels is a powerful tool for traders looking to make informed decisions and maximize their returns. By understanding the strength of levels, different types of levels, and how to use them in trading, traders can improve their overall trading strategy.

Chapter 6

Candlestick and Chart Patterns to Give Confirmation and Confidence to Your Trading

Technical analysis is a widely used method for evaluating securities and making investment decisions.

Chart patterns play a crucial role in this process, as they help traders and investors identify potential price movements and trends. In this chapter, we cover the basics of candlestick charts and various chart patterns that are commonly used in technical analysis. We delve into the following chart patterns: candlestick basics, pinbars, two-candle patterns, tweezer patterns, double tops and bottoms, head and shoulders, and megaphone patterns.

Each pattern is described in detail, including its formation, interpretation, and usage in trading and investing. This chapter is a comprehensive guide for traders and investors who want to master the art of chart pattern analysis and make informed investment decisions.

Traders can utilize repeatable chart patterns to recognize potential entry points in the market. These patterns provide clear indications of when a price is poised to change direction, allowing for informed trading decisions.

I have created a free bonus guide and video course for the readers of this book. All you need to do is go to https:// tradingstrategyguides.com/book to get a free gift and special video message from me thanking you for purchasing this book.

Using candlestick patterns to enter into trades is called *price action trading* because you are only using price as the guide for your entries and exits. This can be an effective way to enter trades because price action trading uses momentum to enter into trades, and that momentum can carry the price farther into more momentum.

One key point I want to mention about using candlestick patterns or candle-by-candle analysis is that you must look at the market as a whole and keep in mind the complete picture. This is called using your setups in context. I believe these patterns do work, but they will not be effective if you do not look at the market as a whole.

We need to use structure and levels for everything (and also trends). This is an important distinction that you need to understand to use these patterns effectively.

Candlestick Basics

In Chapter 5 we studied support and resistance levels. Support and resistance occurs when price stops and reverses. Support and resistance levels form on a micro level on one individual candle. When we look at price on the candlestick level, we are zooming way in to look at just one candle. There are support and resistance candles on individual candles or groups of candles because we are zooming way in to look at the price.

Every candlestick chart has the following four pieces of information:

1. The open price
2. The closing price
3. The high price
4. The low price

Figure 6.1 shows how to read a candlestick.

This visual representation of price, called a candlestick, tells the trader what is happening in the market. When we see many different candlesticks together, different patterns form, which give traders great trade opportunities.

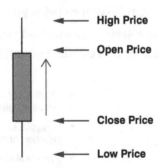

Figure 6.1   Price Data Displayed in Each Candle
SOURCE: TradingStrategyGuides.com.

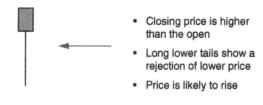

- Closing price is higher than the open
- Long lower tails show a rejection of lower price
- Price is likely to rise

BULLISH PINBAR

Figure 6.2   Bullish Pinbar Is a Bullish Price Action Pattern
SOURCE: TradingStrategyGuides.com.

Next we are going to talk about pinbars. Candles form what is called a pinbar because it looks like a pin on the chart.

Bullish Pinbars

We will start with a *bullish pinbar*. It shows that price attempted to move lower, but that move was rejected, and buyers moved in to push the price up. This bullish candle indicates that price could move higher (see Figure 6.2).

Bearish Pinbar

The *bearish pinbar* is a candle where price attempts to go up but gets rejected quickly. When you see this form on your chart, it is showing downward momentum, so this candle is bearish (see Figure 6.3).

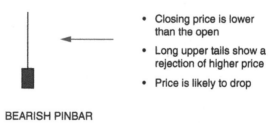

- Closing price is lower than the open
- Long upper tails show a rejection of higher price
- Price is likely to drop

BEARISH PINBAR

Figure 6.3   Bearish Pinbar Closes Below the Open Price
SOURCE: TradingStrategyGuides.com.

Two-Candle Patterns

When you combine two candlesticks you get a great deal of data that gives an indication of which way price could move.

Engulfing Candlestick Patterns

Bullish engulfing candlestick patterns occur when price goes lower and then breaks out past the top of the candle. These are micro levels of support and resistance, and when a price breaks away from these levels, it can signal a potential trend change. As price breaks above the previous candle high, it shows a shift in momentum, breaking the resistance level that was created by the previous candle high point. When you see this type of pattern in conjunction with a trend or key support and resistance level, that creates a high probability trading setup (see Figure 6.4).

The opposite of a bullish engulfing candle is a bearish engulfing candlestick pattern. This happens when price was moving higher but then was rejected to the downside, breaking the lows of the previous candle. This is a bearish price momentum, which could indicate further downward price moves. If you see this

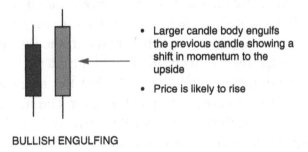

- Larger candle body engulfs the previous candle showing a shift in momentum to the upside

- Price is likely to rise

BULLISH ENGULFING

Figure 6.4   Bullish Engulfing Candle Envelopes the Entire Candle Closing Higher than the Previous Candle

SOURCE: TradingStrategyGuides.com.

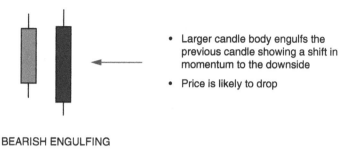

BEARISH ENGULFING

Figure 6.5   Bearish Engulfing Candle Envelopes the Entire Candle Closing
Higher than the Previous Candle
SOURCE: `TradingStrategyGuides.com`.

setup in line with a key support level or trend, it can be a very
good sell trade (see Figure 6.5).

The Morning Star Candlestick Pattern

The morning star candlestick pattern is a bullish reversal pattern
that indicates a potential trend change from bearish to bullish.
It is made up of three candles and is formed after a downtrend.
The first candle is a long dark candle that represents bearish
momentum. The second candle in the figure is a small candle
that is either bullish or bearish, and it is typically referred to as
a "doji" candle because it has no or very little body. This candlestick shows indecisiveness in the market since buying and
selling offset each other. The third candle in the figure is a long
gray candle that represents bullish momentum.

The morning star pattern signals that the bears are losing
control and the bulls are starting to take over. The small doji candle represents indecision or a struggle between the bulls and the
bears, and the long right-hand candle in the figure shows that
the bulls have gained the upper hand. This pattern suggests that
a trend reversal is underway and that traders may look to buy the
security in anticipation of a potential uptrend.

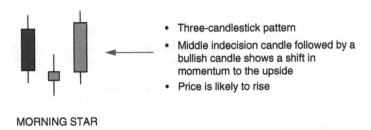

- Three-candlestick pattern
- Middle indecision candle followed by a bullish candle shows a shift in momentum to the upside
- Price is likely to rise

MORNING STAR

Figure 6.6   Morning Star Candlestick Pattern
SOURCE: TradingStrategyGuides.com.

It's important to note that the morning star pattern is only considered valid if it occurs after a downtrend, and if the doji candle is positioned within the body of the first red candle in the figure. Additionally, the right-hand candle in the figure should close above the midpoint of the left-hand candle in the figure to provide further confirmation of a potential trend reversal.

The morning star candlestick pattern is a useful tool for traders to identify potential trend reversals and make informed trading decisions. As with all technical analysis indicators, it should be used in conjunction with other analysis methods to provide a complete picture of market conditions (see Figure 6.6).

The Evening Star Candlestick Pattern

The evening star candlestick pattern is a bearish reversal pattern that signals a potential trend change from bullish to bearish. It is comprised of three candles and is typically formed after an uptrend. The first candle in the figure is long, which represents bullish momentum. The second candle is a small candle that is either bullish or bearish, and it is often referred to as a "doji" candle because it has no or very little body. The third candle is long, which represents bearish momentum.

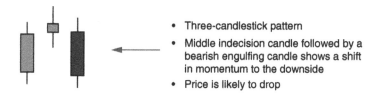

- Three-candlestick pattern
- Middle indecision candle followed by a bearish engulfing candle shows a shift in momentum to the downside
- Price is likely to drop

EVENING STAR

Figure 6.7   Evening Star Candlestick Pattern
SOURCE: TradingStrategyGuides.com.

The evening star pattern signals that the bulls are losing control and the bears are starting to take over. The small doji candle represents indecision or a struggle between the bulls and the bears, and the long right-hand candle in the figure shows that the bears have gained the upper hand. This pattern suggests that a trend reversal is underway, and traders may look to sell the security in anticipation of a potential downtrend.

It's important to note that the evening star pattern is only considered valid if it occurs after an uptrend and if the doji candle is positioned within the body of the first candle in the figure. Additionally, the third candle in the figure should close below the midpoint of the first candle in the figure to provide further confirmation of a potential trend reversal.

The evening star candlestick pattern is a useful tool for traders to identify potential trend reversals and make informed trading decisions. As with all technical analysis indicators, it should be used in conjunction with other analysis methods to provide a complete picture of market conditions (see Figure 6.7).

Tweezer Bottom Patterns

A candlestick pattern that has two bullish pin bars in a row is called a tweezer bottom candle. This is a bullish pattern because the price tried to go down twice and it has been rejected twice

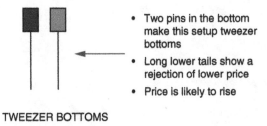

TWEEZER BOTTOMS

Figure 6.8   Tweezer Bottoms Show Price Bouncing off an Area
SOURCE: TradingStrategyGuides.com.

and now we see the price break out of the top, which is breaking a resistance level. If you see this pattern form in conjunction with a key support and resistance level, it is a possible indication that we can see price continue to move higher (see Figure 6.8).

Double and Triple Bottoms and Tops

The double top is a reversal pattern that can be traded on any time frame, but the majority of traders look for those on daily time frames. If you trade this on a shorter time frame, you can use these patterns in the direction of a larger trend (see Figure 6.9).

Figure 6.10 shows another example of a double top that is done in the direction of the current trend.

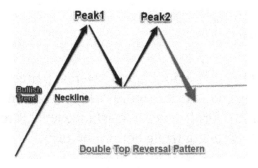

Figure 6.9   Double Top Indicates a Possibility of Price Dropping Further
SOURCE: TradingStrategyGuides.com.

Figure 6.10   Double Top in a Downtrend
SOURCE: TrendSpider.

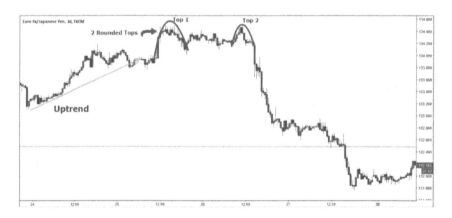

Figure 6.11   Double Top Reversal Pattern
SOURCE: TradingStrategyGuides.com.

Figure 6.11 shows a double top reversal pattern.

A triple top (shown in Figure 6.12) or bottom is when the market hits a support level or a resistance level three times.

Figure 6.13 shows a triple bottom pattern.

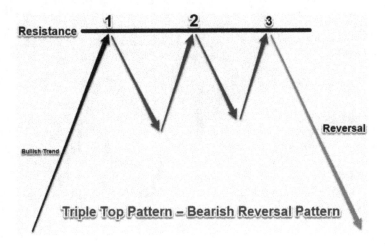

Figure 6.12   Triple Top, Three Rejections of Trend Continuation
SOURCE: TradingStrategyGuides.com.

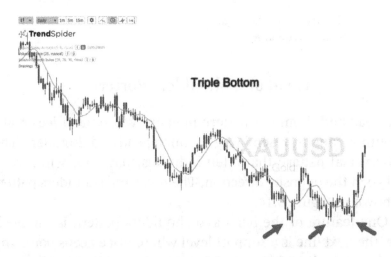

Figure 6.13   Triple Bottom Indicated a Solid Reversal Trade
SOURCE: TrendSpider.

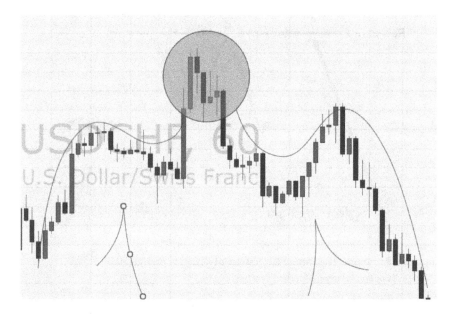

Figure 6.14 Head and Shoulders Pattern
SOURCE: TradingStrategyGuides.com.

Head and Shoulders Pattern

The head and shoulders pattern happens when the price creates an outline roughly resembling a human head and shoulders. This is a reversal pattern that often indicates that price will reverse and go in the opposite direction. The head and shoulders pattern is shown in Figure 6.14.

One feature of the head and shoulders pattern is the neckline; the next line is a support level where price keeps bouncing. The key to trading this pattern is realizing that the neckline support level is no longer going to hold (see Figure 6.15).

The head and shoulders pattern can be traded when the neckline gets broken to the downside (see Figure 6.16).

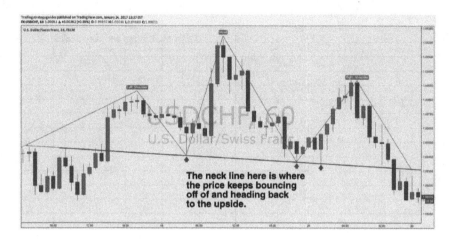

Figure 6.15   Head and Shoulders and Neckline
SOURCE: TradingStrategyGuides.com.

Figure 6.16   Zoomed Out Head and Shoulders Pattern
SOURCE: TradingStrategyGuides.com.

Megaphone Pattern

The megaphone pattern is a consolidation pattern and is found after large price moves. After a large move, price will range and consolidate. This is how a megaphone pattern is formed. This

Figure 6.17   Megaphone Pattern Is a Continuation Pattern
SOURCE: TradingStrategyGuides.com.

pattern can be a high-probability trend continuation pattern. This pattern can also be used to assist traders from getting faked out in breakout trades. Figure 6.17 shows the megaphone pattern.

This pattern is helpful because many traders who want to short the market after a big move end up chasing the market. They sell at the lows and get stopped out because of chasing the market.

Figure 6.18   Using Megaphone Patterns Can Help Avoid a Fake Breakout
SOURCE: TradingStrategyGuides.com.

Waiting for the drop and consolidation period and the forming of the megaphone pattern creates a much higher probability for your trade because of better trading patience.

Breakout traders who try to trade reversals often get trapped because they do not see the megaphone pattern. Train yourself to see this pattern. That will help you avoid getting trapped on fake breakout trades (see Figure 6.18).

The megaphone pattern is one of the best patterns for trading continuations of the trend.

Megaphone Patterns

As a trader, I have found that one of my favorite patterns to trade is the megaphone pattern in conjunction with support and resistance levels. In fact, this pattern has contributed to my longest trading win streak of 22 trades in a row.

I always look for megaphone patterns forming near key support and resistance levels. This allows me to effectively gauge the potential for a trend reversal and execute trades with a higher degree of accuracy. By combining my understanding of market structure, levels, and trend analysis with the clear signals provided by the megaphone pattern, I am able to identify and capitalize on profitable trading opportunities.

In my experience, the megaphone pattern is particularly useful when the market is in a consolidation phase and prices are fluctuating within a narrow range. By recognizing the pattern and taking a position at the right time, I have been able to consistently achieve positive results and grow my trading account.

Trading megaphone patterns in conjunction with support and resistance levels has proven to be a highly effective strategy for me. I will continue to utilize this pattern in my trading and refine my approach for even better results in the future.

Summary

This chapter delves into the various chart patterns commonly used in technical analysis, including candlestick basics, pinbars, two-candle patterns, tweezer patterns, double tops and bottoms, head and shoulders, morning star and evening star patterns, and megaphone patterns. The chapter provides a comprehensive guide for traders and investors who want to master the art of chart pattern analysis and make informed investment decisions.

Each pattern was described in detail, including its formation, interpretation, and usage in trading and investing. The chapter highlights the importance of considering structure, levels, and trends when utilizing chart patterns to make trading decisions. The megaphone pattern, in particular, was highlighted as a highly effective strategy when used in conjunction with support and resistance levels.

This chapter provides a solid foundation for traders and investors who want to incorporate chart pattern analysis into their investment strategy. By mastering these patterns, traders can identify potential market trends and execute trades with a higher degree of accuracy.

Chapter 7

How to Trade with Indicators Using These Tools to Get Laser-Targeted on Your Entry

T rading with technical indicators is a popular strategy used by many traders to make informed decisions about buying and selling securities. In this chapter, we explore the various types of indicators used in trading, including moving averages, relative strength index (RSI), moving average convergence divergence (MACD), overbought/oversold levels, momentum, and divergences.

These indicators are designed to help traders understand the behavior of the market and make predictions about future price movements. By analyzing the signals generated by these indicators, traders can identify trends, momentum shifts, and potential turning points in the market.

This knowledge can be used to make informed decisions about buying or selling a particular security. In this chapter, we delve into each of these indicators, exploring how they are calculated, what signals they generate, and how traders can use them to make better-informed trading decisions.

The Purpose of Indicators

Indicators are useful for scanning for market setups and for gathering additional information on the trades we are trading. In this chapter I teach about some of my favorite indicators and how to use them.

In previous chapters we discovered how to analyze trends, levels, and candlestick patterns. Each additional bit of information we gather gives us better intel to make trading decisions.

I only use three indicators for my trading strategy. The three indicators are the moving average, MACD (moving average convergence divergence), and the RSI (relative strength index).

The first thing you must understand about indicators is that there is no such thing as a perfect indicator. Successful trading is about probabilities and riding out your edge to create long-term gains.

Discipline and risk management are also extremely important to successful long-term trading. In Chapter 11 I teach some important risk management strategies that will guarantee trading success.

Moving Averages

I mentioned the 10 EMA in the trend chapter (Chapter 4) because this indicator is useful in determining current market trends. It is also an important trading indicator, which is why I mention it again here. A *moving average* is the average price of the previous 10 candles. It's called a moving average because every time the price moves the average changes—it adds in the new price and the oldest price drops off.

The *exponential moving average* is a moving average that is more complex, as it gives greater weight to the most recent data.

One great way that I use moving averages is that if the price trades above the moving average, we're in an uptrend. As long as we stay above the exponential moving average, we should expect higher prices. Conversely, if we're trading below, we're in a downtrend. As long as we trade below the moving average, we should expect lower prices.

There is an in-depth article that goes into great detail on how to trade with the exponential moving average on my website TradingStrategyGuides.com.[1]

This indicator is great at finding the trend and finding reversals. My favorite way to trade with the moving average is to find lower time frame reversals and trade them back in the direction of the higher time frame trend.

This has shown to be a high-probability setup over a long period of time (see Figures 7.1 and 7.2).

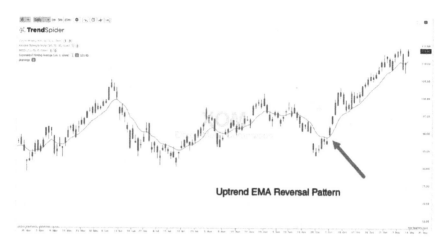

Figure 7.1   Moving Average Breaks Up and a New Trend Begins
SOURCE: TrendSpider.

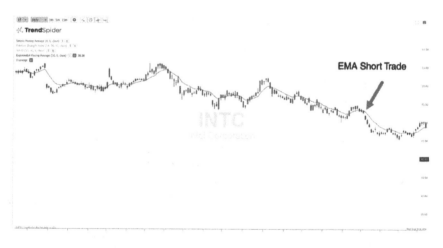

Figure 7.2   EMA Price Breaks Below and a New Downtrend Begins
SOURCE: TrendSpider.

Moving Average Convergence Divergence

The MACD is one of the most popular indicators for traders that comes standard on every single trading platform today. The problem is that most traders do not know how it works or how to trade it.

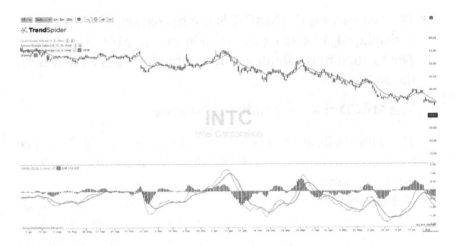

Figure 7.3   MACD Indicator below the Chart
SOURCE: TrendSpider.

The MACD was invented by Gerald Appel over 40 years ago, and people still use this every day in the markets.[2]

The MACD is a separate chart located below the candlestick chart (see Figure 7.3).

There are several important things that MACD can teach you.

First, the MACD includes three exponential moving averages in the indicator: the 26-period EMA, the 12-period EMA, and the 9-period EMA. All of the calculations on the MACD indicator come from these three moving averages.

The MACD indicator is very ingenious in how these moving averages are used, giving many different ways to trade.

Each of these moving averages has a different name. They are called the MACD line, signal line, and histogram.

- The MACD line is located on the MACD chart and is calculated by subtracting the 12 EMA from the 26 EMA.
- The signal line is the 9-period EMA. This is called the signal line because many trading strategies use it when the price crosses the MACD line.

- The last part on the MACD is the histogram. The histogram is displayed as a bar chart inside of the MACD indicator. The histogram is calculated by subtracting the 12 EMA from the 26 EMA.

The MACD chart has additional features:

- The bars are larger or smaller based on how much difference there is between the two indicators. This is a great way to see price momentum.
- If the number is positive, the bar chart is above the 0 line. If the number is negative, the bar chart goes below the zero line.
  Price above the zero line is an indication of bullish momentum, and price below the zero line is bearish momentum.

The histogram and the MACD line are from the same data, but it is displayed differently on the indicator. This is a great way to get a different point of view from the data.

Figure 7.4 shows a detailed image of MACD and all the different components.

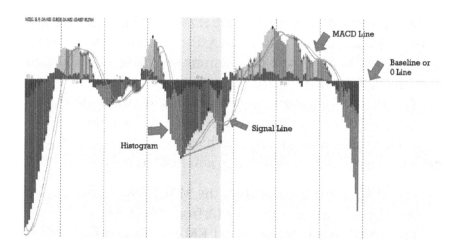

Figure 7.4   Components of the MACD Indicator
SOURCE: TradingStrategyGuides.com.

Multiple Ways to Trade the MACD

There are several ways to trade the MACD. This section discusses convergences, divergences, and zero-line crosses.

Convergences

One of the best ways to trade the MACD is to find *convergence*—when lines meet at a point or when things come together and move together.[3] Convergences can be seen on a chart and mean that price and movement on the indicator are moving together. Figure 7.5 shows how to identify convergences and trade them.

These work well when we trade them with the trend, market levels, and chart patterns. When there are a number of alerts working together, such as price action patterns and indicators, that increases the probability of your trade.

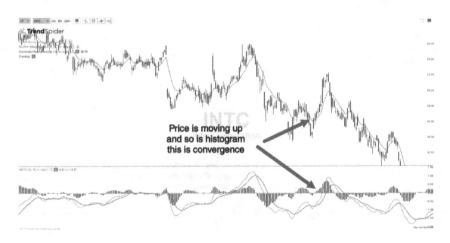

Price is moving up
and so is histogram
this is convergence

Figure 7.5   Convergence on the MACD
SOURCE: TrendSpider.

Divergences

Another great way to trade with the MACD is with divergences. Divergence is when price moves in one direction and the indicator moves in the opposite direction. Many times in trading this indicates that price will begin to trade a reversal (see Figure 7.6).

Notice in the preceding image that price has made a new low, yet the MACD indicator is moving up. This is a clear divergence signal. When you see divergence, it doesn't mean that you automatically take a trade, but it is a signal that a reversal could happen soon and you need to begin getting ready to find an entry position so you're prepared when the reversal happens.

This is why that call is an indicator: when you see it happen, it is an indication that a trade will come very soon.

If there is a strong daily chart trend and you see a divergence happen on a lower time frame such as one hour, it can be a great way to get back into the trend trade in the direction of the trend.

Figure 7.6   Price Moving Down, Indicator Moving Up—This Is Divergence
SOURCE: TrendSpider.

In this image two common signals were false the 10 EMA cross and the zero line cross on the MACD

Figure 7.7 False Signals
SOURCE: TrendSpider.

Figure 7.7 shows an example of the divergence setup. We can see that there were two false indications of a trade: the 10 EMA cross and the zero line cross. You would have lost that trade; however, after the divergence appeared, that is when the winning setup was revealed.

Be patient, and wait for divergence. This is another good way to increase your probability because you are willing to wait for the perfect entry.

Understanding Trading Possibilities with This Trading Strategy

John is a successful trader who relies heavily on technical analysis in his trading strategy. One of his favorite indicators is the moving average convergence divergence (MACD) indicator. John uses the MACD in conjunction with divergence to identify potential trade setups in the direction of the trend.

John found that using divergence with the MACD was an effective way to enter trades. When the MACD showed bullish divergence, he would look for long trade opportunities, and when it showed bearish divergence, he would look for short trade opportunities. By combining the MACD with divergence, John was able to enter trades with a higher degree of confidence, which improved his overall trading performance.

For example, imagine a trader who takes just under four trades per day during the course of a year.

To calculate the profit if they risk $500 on losses but win $1,000 on wins, and they win 59.7% of the time on 987 trades, we use the following formula:

Profit = (Winning trades * Win rate * Win amount) − (Losing trades * Loss rate * Loss amount)

Winning trades = 987 * 59.7% = 588

Losing trades = 987 − 588 = 399

Profit = (588 * 1,000) − (399 * 500) = 588,000 − 199,500 = $388,500

Therefore, the trader would have made a profit of $388,500.

Zero-Line Cross-Entry

Another way to trade the MACD is to trade the zero-line cross.

When price crosses over the zero line and it is going in the direction of the long-term trend, it is a very good signal. This particular setup is also effective when the divergence happens before the zero-line cross (see Figure 7.8).

An effective entry strategy is indicated by the zero-line cross on the MACD (as shown in Figure 7.8). If you trade the zero-line cross in the direction of the overall trend using proper risk management, that can be effective for trading.

Figure 7.8   Arrow Pointed at MACD Zero-Line Cross—A Good Entry Signal
SOURCE: TrendSpider.

Back Test Practice

Do a manual back test for 20 trades as a training exercise. Apply an MACD and 10-period EMA to your charts. Find a trend and journal the results of 20 MACD zero-line cross-trades along with a 10 EMA cross in the direction of the trend and log the results. If you do this often, it will increase confidence in your trading strategy.

RSI Trading Strategy

RSI (relative strength index) was invented by J. Welles Wilder.[3] This indicator is good for finding overbought and oversold conditions as well as finding momentum setups.

The default setting for RSI is *14 period*. This means that the indicator is using the data to gather momentum or relative strength for the last 14 candles on your chart. If you want a faster strength setting, look at a lower number of periods; if you want a slower strength index, use a longer period. Many times I will add a 4-period RSI to my charts; I call this a fast RSI. I also sometimes add a 21 period, which I call a slow RSI.

Overbought and Oversold RSI

RSI is often used as a tool to find out if a stock is overbought or oversold. If the RSI is over 70, you will want to short; if the RSI is under 30, you will want to buy.

This strategy can work, but there are some drawbacks to using this tool for determining if a stock is overbought or oversold.

Here is a list of reasons why it might not be a good idea to use the RSI for this.

1. The 14 period is calculated over 14 candles, which is too short a period of time to determine whether a trend is going to turn around (see Figure 7.9).
2. The overbought and oversold can continue going for months and years, meaning that if you use this to predict a reversal, it is an inaccurate method to do so.

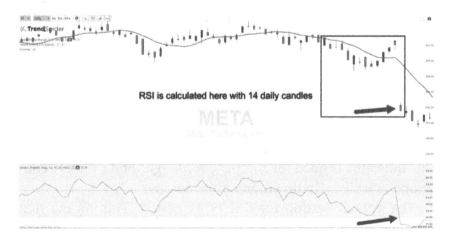

Figure 7.9   RSI Is Calculated during 14 Days (in the Box)
SOURCE: TrendSpider.

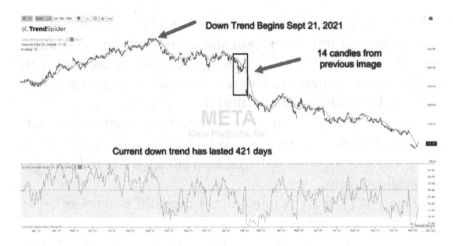

Figure 7.10   RSI Trend Zoomed Out
SOURCE: TrendSpider.

Figure 7.9 shows RSI dropping below 30 after 14 candles. The problem with trying to time a reversal is that 14 candles is not enough time to determine if the price actually resulted from the stock being overbought or oversold. Many traders fall into this trap without understanding the big picture.

Meta (the subject of Figure 7.9) continued to fall an additional $149 dollars or 62%. If you used this as an overbought or oversold indicator to trade, you would have been extremely wrong. The current downtrend on Meta has been going for 421 days. Using an overbought or oversold for that small amount of data does not do an effective job because it is too small a sample size of price data.

Figure 7.10 shows why 14 candles is too small a period in this case.

This price is so bearish, and the RSI shows that well. However, it does not show if a move has ended, so buying just because it is oversold is not a good idea. We need to make sure the bearish move is over before we start looking at buying.

This is why I teach using trends to formulate your entry plans. If you only use RSI overbought and oversold in the same direction of the trend, it works a higher percentage of the time. This is the value of context. An indicator or chart pattern must always be looked at in the context of the greater market.

If you find a trend on a higher time frame such as a weekly or daily, then drop down to a lower time frame for the RSI overbought or oversold position, that is an effective way to find high-probability entries.

Figure 7.11 is an example of an oversold trade that works great in the direction of the trend.

The way to determine the entry is to wait for price to hit a key level, and then when we see price reverse, we get into the trade and put the stop loss below the current support or resistance level.

Using a 10 EMA is a good way to enter the trade, when we get a price move above the 10 EMA with a candlestick pattern forming and a key level. We covered that in detail in previous chapters.

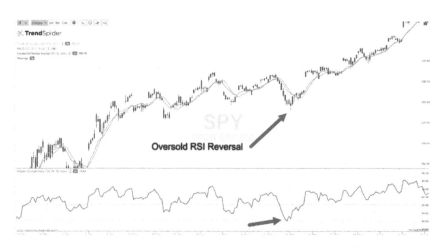

Figure 7.11   Oversold RSI Setting Up a Buy off a Bounce off a Key Support Level
SOURCE: TrendSpider.

In the example shown in Figure 7.11, there is a strong uptrend where price pulls back to the 30 level on the RSI. This is an oversold example of trading on the RSI.

RSI Divergence Explained

As explained in the MACD section of this chapter, divergence is when price hits a new high or low but doesn't make a new high and low on the chart. It is extremely important to understand how that works and why it will help you identify key trade opportunities.

If we are using RSI, we must remember that it is a momentum or strength indicator. The default setting for this indicator is 14. When the RSI is oversold or overbought and gets to over 70, that is on the last 14 candles.

That means that the last 14 candles have been very strong and pushed the RSI over 70. Now if price goes sideways for seven or eight candles, then goes down for four candles but then goes back up to a new high for the last three, then the total RSI will not have much movement during the 14 periods measured.

As mentioned previously in this chapter, the default setting for RSI measures the strength or weakness in the last 14 candles. Figure 7.9 shows massive weakness for all 14 candles. This is a poor way to find a trade alone without using any other data. That is why we need to look at trends, support and resistance levels, and chart patterns, before making any trading decisions.

Divergence is an additional tool we can use in making good trading decisions. RSI divergence is when price goes up but RSI is dropping.

Because RSI is calculated for a small amount of data, the price can go up while RSI is dropping. This can happen because the RATE of increase is dropping, indicating that the bulls are getting tired and we could soon see a price reversal.

Figure 7.12   Two Divergence Setups
SOURCE: TrendSpider.

Of course, price can still continue to go up. Just because we have divergence is not a guarantee of a reversal, but it is an important indication that the momentum is slowing down and we can see a reversal happening (see Figure 7.12).

Figure 7.12 shows that we have price making new lows but the RSI indicator does not; these are two quality divergence trades on one chart.

Divergence is a great tool to give you a visual representation of when the market is slowing down. The best way to trade divergence is when you are using the indicator to spot a reversal in the direction of a trend.

Using RSI as a Momentum Indicator

Another way to use the RSI is momentum rather than overbought and oversold.

Since the default setting on the RSI is 14, you see swings on the indicator occur rather quickly. If you see the RSI cross from

Figure 7.13   RSI Crossing above the 50 Line
SOURCE: TrendSpider.

below the 50 line to above the 50 line, that can be a clear sign that price is changing directions and many times that move can continue to go for a long period of time.

This is using the RSI as a way to enter trades based on momentum rather than using the RSI for overbought and oversold (see Figure 7.13).

Using the RSI as it is crossing the 50 level shows that momentum is rising and it is bullish that price is rising. The momentum surge can continue to carry the price in the direction of the trend. This particular entry method is a later entry than oversold and overbought; however, this can help you avoid trying to pick tops and bottoms, which can be a very low-probability way to trade.

Indicators are a great way to get additional data and insight into your trading process, and using them as I have described can give you the tools you need to pick the best trading setups.

Summary

Trading with indicators is a common approach in technical analysis, which is used to help traders make informed decisions about buying and selling financial instruments. In this chapter, we discussed several popular indicators that traders use in their trading strategies, including moving averages, the moving average convergence divergence (MACD) indicator, overbought and oversold indicators, divergences, the relative strength index (RSI), and RSI momentum strategy.

Moving averages are used to identify trends and to determine whether a financial instrument is in an uptrend or downtrend. A simple moving average is calculated by taking the average of the closing prices over a specified number of periods, while an exponential moving average puts more weight on recent prices.

The MACD is a momentum oscillator that is used to identify potential trend changes. It is calculated by subtracting the 26-period exponential moving average from the 12-period exponential moving average. The MACD also has a signal line, which is a 9-period exponential moving average of the MACD line. The MACD is used to identify bullish and bearish divergences, which can be used as an early warning sign of a potential trend change.

Overbought and oversold indicators, such as the RSI, are used to determine when a financial instrument may be overvalued or undervalued. A financial instrument is considered overbought when its price has risen too high and may be due for a correction, while a financial instrument is considered oversold when its price has fallen too low and may be due for a rebound.

Divergences occur when the price of a financial instrument is moving in one direction, while the indicator is moving in the opposite direction. Divergences can be used as an early warning sign of a potential trend change and can help traders determine whether to enter or exit a trade.

The RSI is a momentum oscillator that is used to determine whether a financial instrument is overbought or oversold. It is calculated by comparing the average gains and losses over a specified number of periods. The RSI is commonly used in conjunction with divergences to confirm trend changes.

Finally, the RSI momentum strategy involves using the RSI to identify potential trade setups. When the RSI crosses above a certain level, it is considered overbought and a potential sell signal. Conversely, when the RSI crosses below a certain level, it is considered oversold and a potential buy signal.

Trading with indicators can be a powerful tool for traders who want to make informed decisions about buying and selling financial instruments. By combining several indicators, such as moving averages, the MACD, overbought and oversold indicators, divergences, the RSI, and the RSI momentum strategy, traders can gain a more complete picture of the market and make more informed trades.

Notes

1. https://tradingstrategyguides.com/exponential-moving-average-strategy/.
2. https://cmtassociation.org/presenter/gerald-appel/.
3. https://www.fidelity.com/learning-center/trading-investing/technical-analysis/technical-indicator-guide/RSI.

Part III

Implement Your Trading Strategy and Achieve Your Goals

Part III of this book is designed to help you turn the knowledge you've acquired in the previous chapters into a successful daily trading routine. Chapters 8 through 12 are filled with practical and actionable steps to help you implement your trading strategy and achieve your goals.

Chapter 8 focuses on the daily trading process, providing a special routine for traders to help them identify and analyze market conditions and make informed decisions.

Chapter 9 covers top-down analysis, a critical component of successful trading, helping you analyze market trends and conditions to make informed decisions about your trades.

Chapter 10 takes the entire trading strategy and puts it all together, helping you find the perfect entries into the market.

In Chapter 11, you will learn about money management, a critical component of any trading plan, including how to assess and manage risk in your trades, and how to protect your capital and maximize your profits.

Finally, Chapter 12 provides a vision and road map for your life and purpose in trading, including setting realistic and achievable trading goals, creating a plan to reach those goals, and staying focused and motivated along the way.

By following the steps outlined in these chapters, you will be well on your way to becoming a successful and profitable trader.

Chapter 8

Daily Trading Process to Create High Performance and Consistency

In every demanding activity that takes a great amount of skill—from sports, to business, to trading—all of the best practitioners use a clearly defined process.

Success in the world of trading often boils down to one simple principle: consistency. The most successful traders are those who are able to maintain a consistent approach to their trading, day in and day out. One of the keys to achieving this consistency is to develop a daily trading process that you repeat over and over again.

As traders, it can be easy to get caught up in the excitement of big trades and large profits. However, it is the little things that we do every day that ultimately determine our success or failure. Focusing on the little things, such as following a daily trading process, can help us increase our capacity for success by establishing a foundation of good habits and a clear mindset.

A daily trading process is simply a set of steps that you follow every day to manage your trades and make informed decisions. This process can include steps such as reviewing market conditions, analyzing data, setting stop losses, and making trades. By following these steps every day, you can build repetition and establish a consistent approach to your trading.

Creating a daily trading process is not difficult, but it does require discipline and a commitment to sticking to the process every day. The first step is to identify the key elements of your trading strategy, such as your risk management approach and the specific indicators that you use to make trades. Next, organize these elements into a step-by-step process that you can follow every day. Finally, make a commitment to following the process every day, even when it feels repetitive or monotonous.

By establishing a daily trading process, you can increase your capacity for success in the world of trading. By focusing on the little things and repeating the same steps every day, you can build repetition, develop good habits, and create a foundation for long-term success.

Consistency Is a Trading Superpower

Being consistent is a superpower in trading. Being consistent is a superpower in life. The people who show up day in and day out, those are the heroes. I have been fortunate to have many people who have impacted me greatly who were consistently there for me in my life.

Consistency means doing the same thing over and over again without fail. If you cannot be consistent, you will not ever accomplish your goals in trading. It is that simple.

> One who is faithful with very little is also faithful with much.[1]

Buttering Your Potatoes

I learned a valuable lesson about the power of doing something small when I was a cook at Ponderosa Steakhouse. The manager who trained me in the kitchen was observing me using the butter scooper and buttering baked potatoes. He noticed that I had thrown a tub of butter into the garbage even though there was a small amount of butter at the bottom of the tub. I did this because the butter scoop was rounded and couldn't scoop out the corners. He explained to me that I was wasting butter, but I replied that it was just a little bit and that it didn't matter. He then took the time to get me a spatula and use that to get the remaining butter out of the tub, which would butter about four additional potatoes.

Then Nick explained that the reason it was important was because of the volume of butter we were using. We were using about 10 tubs of butter a day in the restaurant. If I would take the time to use the spatula and get the remaining butter out of the tub each time, that would allow us to get an extra one tub of butter per day. We bought the butter in cases of 10 tubs per case. Each case was about $100 at the time, about $10 per tub. Using the spatula (which took about 10 seconds) instead of throwing it away saved the restaurant about $300 per month, which equals $3,600 per year and that equals $36,000 per 10 years just by using a spatula in a restaurant.

Now think about this for a minute. If we find just 10 additional small things like scooping butter out of a tub, you have found 10 additional ways to consistently improve performance. By focusing on those 10 little things and doing so consistently, instead of saving $300 a month you can save $3,000 a month or more.

The same thing can be said of trading. If you consistently observe and evaluate your entire process, you will find many ways to improve. This is a massive advantage in trading. Those of you reading this book are willing to do the little things that most people think don't matter when in fact the little stuff is everything.

Do not overlook the small things because they become big things. For example, if you can learn to make $1 a day in the markets, you can learn to make $2 a day. If you can learn to make $2 a day, you can make $10 a day, and if you can make $10 a day, you can make $1,000 a day.

Increase Capacity by Increasing the Size of Your Container

If you have a one-gallon jug and you fill it up with five gallons of water, what happens to the five gallons? One gallon is in the jug, and the rest is spilled all over the floor and wasted.

To grow and expand as a trader you must increase your capacity—your ability to make profits and hold on to them. We expand our capacity by increasing our trading experience. We increase our trading knowledge by learning how to hang on to profits and by learning how to grow our emotional intelligence. It takes personal growth to go from trading a $1,000 account to a $1 million account.

You might think it doesn't matter, but it is a big deal emotionally and to our surroundings.

One of the best ways to increase our capacity and our skills is to create a trading process that puts us in the right frame of mind every day.

In life we experience many ups and downs. One of the reasons this happens is we are not always ready to carry the load we are attempting to carry. If I start making money trading and I make it too fast, it is inevitable that I will crash and burn later on. That happens because I was not ready to do the things necessary to hold on to my profits and trade at that high level.

This is a capacity issue: I need to be able to grow as a trader to handle more profits and learn how to hold on to them. I must grow my skills, my emotions, and my trading knowledge.

I have personally experienced this many times and I have learned that when I have a major setback it is because I am not ready for the level I was at. I need to keep pushing ahead and keep learning and growing so I can get to the next level and stay there.

What Is a Trading Process?

A *trading process* is a step-by-step list of items that you do in a specific order before and during your trading. Creating a process has several advantages that can help you become a trader who consistently makes profits in the markets. The first thing that creating a trading process does is increase awareness of your emotions and mindset. It also creates awareness of what is happening in the markets.

The number of things that a trading process does for a trader is probably too long to list in this book. One vitally important thing, though, that a trading process does is help create consistency, which is the way to begin to build high performance in anything you do.

The next reason for creating a trading process is that it creates the ability to train your brain. We humans are creatures of habit. Our brains are like computers, and creating a trading process trains your mind to move on autopilot.

One example that I often use to explain this is learning to drive. I recently started training my son to drive, and all the memories of when I started driving came flooding back to me.

When you first start driving, everything is scary. Everything is slow, and your brain doesn't have great skills. You might drive into the middle lane or even off the side of the road. You have to think about every decision you make. Most car accidents happen with teenagers who are first starting to drive.[2]

But after driving for 30 years now I don't have to think about what I am doing. It's become automatic.

This is what creating a trading process does for us in trading. It is a program that becomes automatic.

If we do not do things the exact same way each time, we can't get the automatic skills to help us to trade automatically. Repetition also helps to speed up the learning process to get you to trading successfully much faster.

Another great benefit to creating a trading process is that it gives you a clear way to measure your performance. The process defines the things that you need to measure. It creates a review process and incorporates a way to review each step of the way each day. You can measure your trade entries; you can measure your daily emotions, your physical body, how you feel, if you give yourself proper nutrition and sleep. You can also measure your profits when using a daily trade process because you can give yourself the time you need to be able to systematically review each step.

Many traders just jump right into trading because of fear of missing out (FOMO). Fear makes them feel that they don't have time to create a process and do not have time to review their trading. This is not the path to success. There is always time to review and always time to work on yourself. If you do not make the time to develop and use the process, you will not improve.

An additional benefit is increased focus. What you think about is what you will do, and having a process helps to build your attention and daily focus on the trading process, which will help you grow consistently.

John Assaraf, who is well known for his study of the brain and his massive success in business, says that the brain prioritizes what we put the majority of our focus on (see Figure 8.1).[3]

The last benefit of having a trading process is that it gives you the tools and foundation you need to achieve constant improvement. If we improve a little bit each day, then over time that equals massive growth and this is the way to become a seven-figure trader and beyond.

Figure 8.1   John Assaraf Teaching on the Power of the Brain
SOURCE: Twitter.

One of the people who has helped me build my own process is Stacey Burke, who was a guest on the *How to Trade It* podcast.[4] I learned a great deal from Stacey about how he built a seven-step process for trading. His insight has been invaluable, assisting me to build a great trading process for myself.

How to Create a Trading Process to Constantly Improve

The first thing you need to create a trading process is a list of all the areas that are important to your performance and to make sure you include those areas in your daily review process.

Here is a list of the things that I include in my daily trading process. I recommend that you consider each one of these things when preparing your own daily trading process.

- **Mindset Prep:** Your mind is important so have a plan to keep yourself focused and growing. I include daily reading, prayer, and journaling to keep myself on the path.
- **Focus:** Where you put your attention is where your mind goes to work at automatically improving.
- **Nutrition and Hydration:** Most trading books do not talk about this but it is so important. Every major system in our body needs water to function properly, and if you are not hydrated, then your performance will drop dramatically. If you want to be your best, you need to drink enough water. Food is fuel, and if we put the wrong fuel into our bodies, it will cause you to perform at a much lower level. Monitor what you eat and feed yourself like the winner that you are. Plus it is a major bonus because this will carry over into your health for the rest of your life, which will dramatically improve the quality of your life.

- **Exercise:** Yes exercise! If we are to be trading our best, our bodies have to be strong, and it is proven that the best business people and traders are getting exercise. Richard Branson, one of the most successful businesspeople, says, "I wouldn't be able to achieve all the things I was trying to achieve in my life if I wasn't at the peak of fitness."[5]
  - I personally get some of my best ideas when I am running. I'm not sure why that is, but after a long run I always sit down with a pad and paper and try to write down all the ideas that came to me during a run.
  - Here is a quick list of benefits of exercise.
    - Keeps weight lower.
    - Improves brain function.
    - Improves immune system and fights disease.
    - Improves your mood and emotions.
    - Helps you to get better sleep.
    - Gives you more energy.
    - It adds a level of fun in your life. It is amazing that we can forget how important it is to keep life fun and make sure we add an element of fun to our life on a regular basis. It is a massive way to improve performance.[6]
- **Sleep:** Sleep is one of the most important things that our body needs to keep going strong as we age. Make sure that you find a way to keep your sleep good. Your trading and your life depend on it. Include this in your trading process. You might not think it will make you a better trader, but it absolutely will.
- **Emotions:** Understanding and managing emotions in your trading is critical, because if you are led by negative emotions, you will never be consistent, because following fear and greed will cause you to trade erratically.
- **Trade setups and daily plans:** Make sure you know exactly what trade you are looking for each day, find the best setup

you can, and trade that each day. Have a clear description of that trade setup defined in your daily trade process. This book is going to help you define the setup. Review Part II, Chapters 5 through 8, the trading strategy sections.

- **Review periods:** I have multiple review periods each day.
  - I review my process before I trade.
  - I do a quick review after each trade.
  - I do a review at the end of each trading session.
  - I do a review at the end of each week.
  - I do a monthly review.
  - I do a yearly review.

It might seem very intimidating to do this review process, but it actually doesn't take a long time. A review could take as little as five minutes to go over some of these things, but the key is that it helps me to maintain focus and consistency. I also am often changing, upgrading and improving my process as I go along. I write down why I am changing it and then record how that change has improved or changed my results.

I have a personal daily process checklist that I use for my trading. I have printed this list and I laminate it and leave it next to my desk while I am trading. You can access this pdf file at https://tradingstrategyguides.com/book. This is a special bonus for you since you purchased this book.

If we do not record how the results of the change help or hurt us, we do not know if the changes were helpful or if they actually hurt our performance.

Creating a trading process is something that takes time and effort to do on the front end, but the results it yields are more than worth it in the long term. I recommend that, after reading this chapter, you take some time to think about it and take action to create your own daily trading process.

Summary

In this chapter, we discussed the importance of consistency in the world of trading and how developing a daily trading process can help traders achieve this consistency. We discussed the key elements of a successful daily trading process, including steps such as reviewing market conditions, analyzing data, setting stop losses, and making trades.

The chapter emphasized the importance of focusing on the little things in trading, such as following a consistent approach to managing trades and making informed decisions. By repeating the same steps every day, traders can build repetition, establish good habits, and increase their capacity for success.

We also discussed the benefits of creating a daily trading process, including increased consistency, discipline, and a clearer mindset. We provided tips for creating a daily trading process, such as identifying the key elements of your trading strategy, organizing these elements into a step-by-step process, and committing to following the process every day.

The power of consistency in trading cannot be overstated. By developing a daily trading process and focusing on the little things, traders can increase their capacity for success and achieve their long-term goals in the world of trading.

Notes

1. https://www.biblegateway.com/passage/?search=Luke%2016%3A10&version=ESV.
2. https://www.morrisbart.com/faqs/what-age-group-has-the-most-accidents.
3. https://twitter.com/johnassaraf/status/1580727405102391296.
4. https://podcast.tradingstrategyguides.com/stacey-burkes-forex-trading-strategy/.
5. https://www.inc.com/jackelyn-ho/this-is-what-richard-branson-told-me-about-exercise.html.
6. https://www.mayoclinic.org/healthy-lifestyle/fitness/in-depth/exercise/art-20048389.

Chapter 9

How to Form a Daily Trade Plan: Preparing for Market Success

As a trader, you are always on the lookout for ways to stay ahead of the market and make informed decisions that can yield profitable outcomes. One of the key approaches to achieving this goal is conducting a daily top-down analysis. This analysis involves breaking down the market into smaller parts, starting with the big picture, and working your way down to the individual securities that you trade. The aim is to identify trends and determine how they are affecting different sectors and individual stocks.

In this chapter, we will explore the concept of top-down analysis and its importance in the world of trading. We will cover the different steps involved in conducting a daily top-down analysis, including the analysis of macroeconomic indicators, industry trends, and individual stocks.

By the end of this chapter, you will have a deeper understanding of how to use top-down analysis to make informed trading decisions, increase your chances of success, and stay ahead of the market.

Every single day I approach the market the exact same way to come up with my trading plan for that day.

I have said it many times and will continue to say it: the more we are willing to prepare, the greater skills we'll have, and that sets us apart from other traders, who are not willing to do what we will do.

My ideal trading scenario is what I call "one and done." I like to analyze the market and make one good trade and then be done for the day. If I do it well, I can have a 30-minute day and then be done trading for the day, and I will have the rest of the day to enjoy my time.

Think about this for a moment: I have laid out a ton of prep work, which seems like a lot, and it can be at times. But if you do all that work and you actually only have to trade 30 minutes per day, that is a dream lifestyle that allows you to make a good revenue and also do the things that you enjoy with your life.

The value of preparation cannot be overstated, and in trading preparation is extremely important. Colin Powell said: "There are no secrets to success. It is the result of preparation, hard work, and learning from failure."[1] This is why each day before making my trade I do my prep work. I first review my daily trading process as outlined in Chapter 8.

Start with Weekly Charts

I first review the weekly charts each day and begin to formulate a plan on how I think the price is going to be moving this week. I look at the weekly highs and lows, and I mark those on my charts. These weekly highs and lows work as support and resistance levels. Weekly levels are stronger than lower time-frame levels because weekly is a larger time frame and has more price data included in the charts.

This helps me create something called a *daily bias*. This helps me know what direction I want to trade each day.

Next I look at the previous week's highs and lows and mark those on my charts. I analyze the trends and diagonal levels and annotate them on the charts.

One trick I use to help me identify the levels is for weekly charts; I use blue lines on my chart so I know that all my levels that are weekly are blue. This is part of my system, so I can always be aware of the stronger levels because of color coding.

Daily Levels Are the Next Part of My Daily Trading Process

I then begin to zoom in and go to the daily charts. I take what I have discovered on the weekly charts and analyze the daily to see if my ideas are strengthened. I look at the same levels that I do on the weekly. I see the current daily high and low, and the previous high and low, and I mark those levels on the charts. If the daily and weekly highs are at the same level, I mark those because that makes them even stronger.

I then begin to formulate different entry strategies based on what I see on the daily and weekly charts.

What I primarily look for is pullbacks in the direction of the overall trend and direction in which I believe the weekly chart is going to go. This concept is explored in Chapter 4 regarding trends.

Fifteen-Minute Charts for the Entry

After that I look at the weekly and daily charts and formulate the plan. I go to the 15-minute charts for my entry. I begin watching price, and if the price does exactly as I expect, I will make my trade on the 15-minute charts.

The reason I use the 15-minute charts is because this method has proven to work for me, and it works well for the time of day when I do a lot of trading. There is not a secret entry or better entry on the 15-minute time frame. This is just what works for me right now based on the time I have allotted for trading. There is no correct time frame or entry time frame that will give you an edge. There are pros and cons with each time frame you use. Remember, the higher the time frame, the more data for your decision making. Therefore a higher time frame gives you better analysis.

Yes, I am looking at a 15-minute chart, but I am using the weekly as my guide. In fact, I do not even consider that I am trading on the 15-minute because I am using data gathered from many different time frames to make my trading decisions.

I recommend that you choose a trading time of day and time frame that helps advance your quality of life. We trade so that we can live a better life. We do not live to trade.

Some traders use weekly and daily, and others use hourly and 5-minute. It depends on your personality and trading preference.

I approach the markets the same way each and every day, and this is so important for helping me develop marketing consistency.

Ups and Downs Are Part of Trading

The daily focus of having a trade plan and trade process will keep you strong during the ups and downs on your journey to becoming a profitable trader. My goal is to help traders be aware of these difficult times by sharing some of these methods to help them not quit.

One of the biggest confidence boosters for a trader is when they face many losses in a row and despite incredible setbacks they stick with it and have success over adversity.

Adversity is one of our biggest friends and allies if we realize it before we get into a large drawdown. We learn to overcome obstacles, and when we do, we know that we will never fail if we do not quit.

It took me a long time to become successful. Two things helped me tremendously to become a successful trader.

1. Not quitting and developing perseverance. There were so many times I could have quit but refused to, even though many times the journey was quite painful. I have never met a trader who did not have to go through this process.
2. Developing my daily process. I understood the rules of trading and had great skills, but it wasn't until I built my daily trading process that I found true success. The daily process is something that you should pay attention to.

For a long time I did not take creating a daily process seriously, but the lack of a trading process was the very thing that held me back for such a long time.

I now have a tremendous belief in trading and this process because I have come back from early setbacks and now have a long track record of success.

Summary

This chapter highlights the significance of daily top-down analysis in the trading process. It emphasizes the use of weekly, daily, and 15-minute charts to support the analysis and make informed trades. I provide a detailed explanation of how to carry out this type of analysis, including step-by-step instructions for incorporating different time frames into the analysis.

If they use this approach, traders can gain a more comprehensive understanding of market conditions and make better trading decisions. The chapter also highlights the benefits of consistency and discipline in using this method, as well as the need for continuous learning and improvement.

This chapter emphasizes the importance of incorporating daily top-down analysis into a trading routine in order to make more profitable trades. I provide a clear and comprehensive guide for traders to follow, including the benefits and steps involved in building your own daily process.

Note

1. https://everydaypower.com/preparation-quotes/.

Chapter 10

How to Find Entries: High Performance with Everything Working Together

N ow the moment you have all been waiting for: the complete trading strategy that I use to pull out consistent gains in the market, week in and week out.

In the previous chapters, we learned about the various components of a successful trading system, including trends, support and resistance, indicators, and chart patterns. Now it's time to put all of these pieces together and create a complete trading system. This chapter walks you through the process of creating a step-by-step entry method that incorporates everything we have learned thus far.

Trading can be a challenging endeavor, but by having a well-defined system in place, you can make informed decisions and increase your chances of success. A complete trading system should take into account all of the relevant information available to you, including market trends, support and resistance levels, and technical indicators. By considering all of these factors, you can create a more comprehensive picture of the market and make more informed trading decisions.

In this chapter, we will cover the following topics in detail:

- Understanding the role of trends in a trading system
- Identifying support and resistance levels and incorporating them into your trading strategy
- Using technical indicators to confirm trends and provide additional insight into market conditions
- Incorporating chart patterns into your trading system

By the end of this chapter, you will have a solid understanding of how to put together a complete trading system that incorporates all of the components we have discussed in previous chapters. This system will provide you with a roadmap to help guide your trading decisions and increase your chances of success.

This is going to seem like a review because I have spent so much time building the components of this strategy, but now we are going to put everything together to create the step-by-step strategy.

If you follow this strategy with good money management and trading discipline, you will be on your way to becoming a consistently profitable trader.

The Complete Strategy

This section lays out the steps that make up the complete strategy.

Step 1: The first thing to do is to set up your charts. I use a chart with three indicators:
1. 10 EMA
2. MACD default settings
3. RSI 14

These indicators can be found on any charting platform and will come standard with any broker's charting platform.

Step 2: Go through your daily process.

I always go through the daily process I described in Chapter 8. I do this to keep me mentally, emotionally, and physically sharp. I have to keep my edge at all times when trading. You have to be intentional to be your best each and every day.

This daily process is not the trading system. This is the process that I mentally go through each day to keep myself sharp and to avoid self-sabotage.

I call it the Daily System for High Performance and Consistency:

1. Daily routine (complete before trading).
   - Reading; prayer, meditation; exercise; proper amount of sleep
   - Planning—nutrition, hydration
2. Mindset checklist.
   - Emotions
   - Gratitude
   - Beliefs
   - Intentions for today's session
3. Check news on Forex Factory. I make sure I don't trade during a news announcement.
4. Create daily bias for three trading pairs each day.
5. Create a trade plan for each pair each day.
6. Execute trades according to plan.
7. Review trades at the end of each trading session.
8. Complete an in-depth review once a week.
9. Complete an in-depth review once per month and set 30-day goals. These would not be monetary goals but goals in how you maintain your positive trading habits and processes.
10. Review high-performance processes every 30 days, to see if you would benefit from any updates to the daily process.

Step 3: Identify the trend.

Always identify the trend, and the best setups are trades taken in the direction of the trend. This can be done on any timeframe. I like to identify higher time frame trends and take reversals on the lower time frames to get more targeted entries.

Step 4: Identify key levels.

Mark down and review all the levels each and every day. Identify weekly, daily, and 15-minute levels on the charts. Always look at the previous day's highs and lows. The reason I am identifying these is because the highest probability trades happen on reversals that occur on previous levels.

Step 5: Check indicators.

I am looking at the 10-period EMA for a cross above or below for a high probability entry in the direction of the trend off of a key level. I will also look for a MACD cross where the price will cross over the zero line. Additional items I am looking for are MACD and RSI divergence and overbought and oversold conditions on the RSI. For me to enter a trade, I do not need everything on this list, but I am trying to find the best setup I can and trade that. The more factors that are available in any given trade, the higher the probability.

Step 6: Price and candlestick patterns.

The last piece of information that I am looking for in determining the trade entry is the candlestick pattern. The success rate of these patterns when traded standalone are good, but when you add these to the additional data on the charts it's even better.

Some of the patterns I like to look for are the morning star and evening star, double and triple bottoms and tops, as well as bullish and bearish engulfing candles. My favorite pattern is the megaphone pattern because it helps me fight against fake breakouts.

Step 7: Enter trade.

After all the analysis has been done, I will enter the trade when it fits all of the criteria that I have determined will give me the highest-probability setup. Just like a detective at a crime scene, I am trying to build evidence. The more evidence I find, the better my trade will be.

The last step, trade management, picks up later in this chapter. Hang in there!

Figures 10.2, 10.2, and 10.3 show solid setups according to my strategy. Figure 10.1 shows a trade that has four elements, which is the minimum I look to trade: trend, MACD cross, EMA cross, and double-bottom candlestick pattern. This is a high-probability setup that fits perfectly into my trading system.

Figure 10.2 is an example of a high-probability setup that occurred on bitcoin. Not everything happened all at once. First, we saw the price get oversold, which is an indication that we are going to reverse. There was a double-bottom chart pattern. Then we had the trend line break to the upside and the horizontal level break, along with the EMA cross. All of these factors were working together to create a great trade.

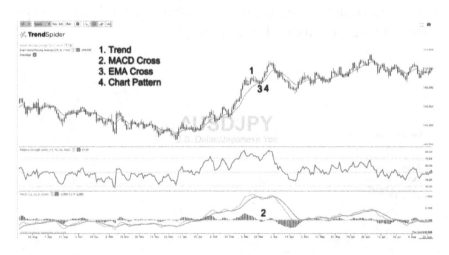

Figure 10.1   Four Confirming Factors of a Trade
SOURCE: TrendSpider.

Figure 10.2   Six Confirmations to Take a Trade
SOURCE: TrendSpider.

Remember to always put the stop loss below the previous candle low, where number 4 is on the chart.

Figure 10.3 shows you exactly what we are looking for with this strategy. There are six key elements in this trade setup, and when you have that many areas working in your favor, it helps increase your probability for trading.

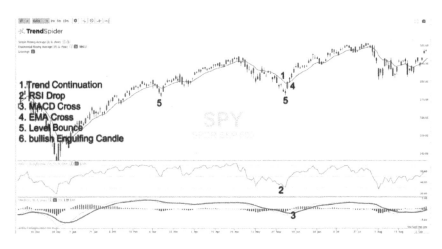

Figure 10.3   Six Trade Confirmations
SOURCE: TrendSpider.

The biggest problem is that you do not always get great setups that look this good, so you have to wait for them or look at lower time frames for these trades to develop.

Breakouts and Reversals

When you are on a level, the market often will shop around before deciding which way it will ultimately go. There are different ways to trade these levels. I prefer to take trend trades and reversals and breakouts in the direction of the trend. However, with breakouts and reversals these trades can be so precise and laser focused that these trades can be highly effective when trading with the trend or countertrend.

When trading around key levels there are two things that the market will do. Since there are only two, we have only two decisions to make, so we have a 50% chance of getting it right.

1. Breakouts
2. Bounce and reverse

Breakouts are great trades, because when a breakout happens the market can run and run and run, and you can get massive return on investment when the breakout occurs (see Figure 10.4).

Those trades are amazing, and if you can learn to get them, you will be an extremely profitable trader. I am going to show some tips here on how to get the breakout trades.

- **Powerful momentum:** When you see a real breakout, it will happen with a great deal of power and force. These are the ones you want to trade.
- **Retest:** If you see a strong breakout, there is usually a retest of the breakout level. This is the time to get into the trade.

Figure 10.4   Great Example of a Breakout
SOURCE: TrendSpider.

- **Do not chase price:** Fear of missing out (FOMO) on breakout trades is the biggest thing we need to fight against. Most
  traders know that breakout trades are extremely profitable
  and that we want to trade them, so we will chase the entry.
  Chasing the entry is when you buy at the very high. I do not
  want to buy at the high. I always let the breakout prove itself
  by doing a retest first.
- **Look for a rising channel:** Many breakout trades have
  an upward rising channel because a rising trend can give
  momentum to break a new price level.

Notice in Figure 10.5 that after the initial breakout, the price
had a retest and came back to the 10 EMA before continuing on
the rest of the way. In this situation, you could have entered the
trade on the initial breakout, or you could have waited until the
retest. This is why we do not need to have fear of missing out on
any trades.

Figure 10.5   Great Breakout Example
SOURCE: Trend Spider.

Fake Break and Reversals

Since the power of the breakout is so strong the fake break and reversal trade is one of the best trades that experienced traders can take advantage of. One of the best times that these happen is on market opens. If the previous day's trading was bullish, most of the traders are thinking that this will continue. The market will go for a break, and then the next candle will be a hard reversal. This is how traders get trapped, and that is where we want to enter the trade.

In the trade example shown in Figure 10.6, the breakout happened but it did not follow through. Instead it reversed. This can be a great setup on its own for the trader who is ready for it. As soon as the failure happens, it can be a great opportunity to take a short trade.

Figure 10.6   There Was a Fake Breakout before the Real One
SOURCE: TrendSpider.

A short trade, also known as short selling or simply short-ing, is a type of trade in which an investor sells a security that they do not own, with the hope of buying it back later at a lower price. In a short trade, the investor bor-rows the security from a broker and sells it on the market, hoping that the price will decrease. If the price does fall, the investor can buy back the same number of shares at the lower price, return the borrowed shares to the broker, and pocket the difference as profit.

One way to help avoid being trapped by fake breakouts is to draw the diagonal trendline on the top of your candles. This is a megaphone pattern and can be a huge help to stop those pesky fake trades that plague so many traders (see Figure 10.7).

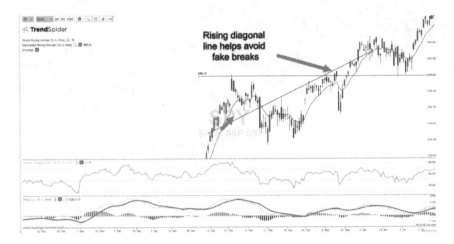

Figure 10.7   Rising Diagonal Trend Is Helpful for Identifying Potential Fake Breakouts
SOURCE: Trend Spider.

Step 8. Trade management.

Once you enter a trade there are many different strategies to manage the trade. I use a dynamic approach to managing the trade. These are discussed in the next sections.

Take-Profit Levels and Stop Loss

A take profit is where you are looking to get out of the trade by hitting the maximum profit. Two things we want to focus on are risk-to-reward ratio and key support and resistance areas.

I want to get as much profit compared to my risk as I can. The bigger the risk-to-reward ratio the better. Also, I like target support and resistance levels to place my take-profit levels because these are areas where price will often turn around.

Once I enter the trade, I am actively managing the trade. My initial goal on any trade is a 2-to-1 risk-to-reward ratio. A risk ratio of 2 to 1 means that I am going to try to make $2 for every $1 that I risk.

Figure 10.8 Range Trading Place Stop below Support
SOURCE: TrendSpider.

We get into risk management in greater detail in Chapter 11.

Figure 10.8 shows that my entry would be on the reversal candle at about $107.50, and my stop loss would have been $104.21, which is a risk of $3.29. The take profit is $120, which means my profit would be $12.5, which is a risk to reward of 3.8 to 1. This means that if I continue winning trades like that, I can be profitable if I only win 25% of my trades.

Managing the Trade Once It Is Open

Since I do not like a profitable trade turning against me—to turn into a loser—I try to move my stop to break even very quickly. When the trade is 40% of the way to the target, I then move my stop loss to the point where I entered the trade. This is called moving the stop to break even.

After I move my stop to break even, I watch the trade, and as it gets close to the target I turn on an auto-trailing stop loss.

A trailing stop loss is a type of order that is used to manage an open position in the market. It is a dynamic order that adjusts the stop-loss price as the market price of the security changes. Unlike a traditional stop-loss order, which is set at a fixed price, a trailing stop loss follows the market price of the security and moves with it in the desired direction, while maintaining a specific distance from the current market price.

For example, if an investor has a long position in a stock and sets a trailing stop loss of 5%, the stop-loss price will move up with the stock price as it rises, but will remain 5% below the current market price. If the stock price then falls, and reaches the stop-loss price, the order will be executed, and the position will be closed.

Trailing stop-loss orders can be useful for investors who want to limit their potential losses while also allowing for potential profits. By adjusting the stop-loss price based on market movements, trailing stop-loss orders help to protect gains and limit losses in volatile markets. This is helpful with trade management and helps me get better trading performance. It is important to test different trailing-stop strategies to help you determine what works best for you.

In the trade example shown in Figure 10.9, I move my stop to break even when I am in profit about $5 per share, which is roughly 40% of my target. Then as it gets close to the target, I slowly lock in my stop to hang on to more of my profits as time goes on. I work hard at being consistent with managing my trades. This helps me avoid drawdowns and also to keep my confidence up and profits continually growing.

Figure 10.9   Hitting Take Profit Near the Top of the Range
SOURCE: TrendSpider.

Summary

A complete trading strategy involves multiple elements, including entry methods, trade management, and exits. When putting together a trading strategy, it's important to focus on identifying entry signals that can provide high-probability trades with favorable risk-reward ratios.

One effective method of identifying trades is by using technical analysis to identify trends, support levels, chart patterns, and indicators. Trend analysis involves looking at price charts to identify the overall direction of the market, while support and resistance analysis involves identifying levels where the price is likely to stall or reverse. Chart patterns, such as head and shoulders or double tops and bottoms, can also provide trade signals. Technical indicators, such as moving averages, and RSI, can be used to confirm trade signals and help with timing.

Another entry method is to look for breakouts, which occur when the price of a security moves beyond a key level of support or resistance. Breakouts can indicate a change in market sentiment and can provide an opportunity to enter a trade in the direction of the break.

Range trading is another entry method that involves identifying a range-bound market, where the price of a security is moving between defined levels of support and resistance. In a range-bound market, traders can look for opportunities to buy at support or sell at resistance.

Trade management is an ongoing process that involves adjusting and monitoring trades as market conditions change. This can include adjusting stop-loss levels, taking profits, or adjusting position size to manage risk exposure. A well-executed trade management plan can help to improve the performance of a trading strategy and increase the chances of long-term success.

Chapter 11

Risk Management Strategy for Trading Mastery

R isk management is an essential part of trading that can mean the difference between success and failure. The goal of risk management is to keep losses small and eliminate drawdowns, allowing traders to remain in the game and continue to grow their trading capital over time. By keeping losses small and controlled, traders are able to handle the ups and downs of the market, reducing the effect of short-term losses.

At the same time, risk management helps traders to focus on fast and safe growth, which allows them to take advantage of winning trades that are larger than what they lose. By following a risk management strategy, traders are able to manage their trades in a disciplined and systematic manner, which helps to eliminate the impact of emotions and personal biases on their trading decisions.

By following a risk management strategy, traders can increase their chances of success and achieve their financial goals over the long term. Whether you are a seasoned trader or just starting out, understanding and applying the principles of risk management is essential to your success in the markets.

What Is Risk Management?

Risk management in trading is the process of identifying, assessing, and controlling risk of an investment's capital and returns. The purpose of risk management is to minimize the losses that result from adverse trades in the financial markets, and to ensure that the investment portfolio is able to generate consistent returns.

The risk management process involves several steps, including:

1. **Identifying the risks:** This step involves identifying different types of risks that are associated with an investment, such as market risk, credit risk, liquidity risk, and portfolio risk.
2. **Assessing the risks:** This step involves evaluating the impact of each risk, as well as determining the level of risk tolerance for the portfolio.
3. **Controlling the risks:** This step involves creating strategies to control the risks identified in the previous steps. This can involve diversifying the investment portfolio, hedging against certain risks, and setting stop-loss orders to limit losses.
4. **Monitoring the risks:** This step involves regularly monitoring the performance of the trades and the impact of any risk management strategies implemented.

Risk management is a critical component of successful trading. It helps to ensure that investments are protected against unexpected events—also called black swan events—and that the portfolio is able to generate consistent returns over time.

This is a complex topic—there is a great deal of study that can be done on risk management. However, I am going to keep it simple because if you make it too complicated, it will be harder to implement into your day-to-day trading.

Mastering risk management is the key to successful trading, and these methods I am teaching are simple to follow. With proper risk management, you can apply just about any strategy and increase your chances of success, regardless of the market conditions or the trading strategy you implement.

Risk management is protecting your capital. Proper risk management is done by knowing at all times exactly how much risk you have before you ever enter the markets.

Failure to take the time to have a risk management plan has destroyed thousands of traders, businesses, and the personal finances of individuals.

It is more fun to think about what you will make than what you could lose, but smart traders first think about what they can lose.

Risk management is one of the most important parts of trading. In this chapter, I teach my risk management strategy and give you several other ideas that you can use for your own trading.

There are several important rules of risk management that you must learn to help you become a successful trader and that are also among the hardest skills to master because it requires self-discipline.

Read and apply the lessons in this chapter often, especially when you are stuck or having a hard time with your success, to get out of any trading problems you are having.

Keep Your Losses Small

The first rule is to keep your losses small and work on making your winnings large. "Lose Small and Lose Fast" is a motto that traders need to remember at all times.

One of my business mentors, Vinney Fisher, CEO of Fully Accountable, taught me that in business one must hire slow and fire fast. What this means is to take your time to make sure you get the right person for the job. Because if you get the right person, that person will help your company grow.

What that means for trading is to take your time finding the right trade, because it will be worth the extra time finding the trade that will pay off for you.

Also we must learn how to cut that trade fast, because the damage to your trading account will be minimal if we do this. It is a trading skill that is difficult to learn but once learned will help your trading account grow extremely fast.

Mark Minervini, who wrote several trading books including *Think and Trade Like a Champion*, says that if you don't take small losses, you will eventually take the mother of all losses.

Something I learned reading about Paul Tudor Jones, one of the most famous and successful traders today, says that if a trade makes you feel uncomfortable, get out of that trade because you can always get back in. Holding on to losers doesn't feel good and can cause anxiety, so rather than carrying that unease in your body just close the trade and find a better one. If you can master this, you will be on your way to trading success.

This can be challenging in trading because the market is always chopping, which makes it difficult to hang on to larger wins. This is where practicing trade management techniques comes into play. This is important for many reasons:

- Cutting off losers early allows you to stop a loser before it gets too big.

Lessons from Observing Many Traders

Here is a powerful story about how important it is to cut the loser early before it becomes a big loser. I own a prop trading company called Trading Strategy Guides Prop Firm. A prop firm is a test that traders take to qualify to trade with company funds. If a trader takes the test and makes a 10% return on investment *before* they lose 5%, they qualify to trade with company money up to $1 million. Here is how it works: if you have a $100,000 test account and make $10,000, you pass because that is 10%. If you lose $5,000 you fail because that is 5%. It is that simple.

This is a great deal for traders because they get to trade with capital they would never have access to otherwise. The entire prop firm thought process is to help traders increase their discipline and manage risk better. You can learn about how you can take a prop test at TradingStrategyGuides.com.

When a trader fails the prop test, I review their trades to help them understand why they failed. There is a repeating pattern with traders who fail.

What I have discovered by reviewing hundreds of traders' prop firm test results is:

- They will trade well for a period of time, but inevitably there is one big trade that gets away from them and becomes a massive loser. That massive loser is the reason they fail the test: it causes them to go above the 5% drawdown.
- If that one big trade had been avoided, they would never have experienced the big drawdown. The simple fact of cutting losers eliminates most trading failures. However, this is easier said than done because no one wants to lose any trades at all—so they hang on hoping that a bad trade will turn around.

- Cutting losers early makes it easy to come back the next day.

  I like to keep my losses small, so that if I have a losing day it is easy to come back. It is not possible to win every single day in trading, no matter how good a trader you are. So when you have a losing day, why not make it small? It is much easier to come back from a small losing day than from a big losing day. This is great for keeping your equity curve moving in the right direction.

- Cutting losses early helps to avoid big drawdowns.

  A big extended drawdown can destroy a trader's equity curve. An *equity curve* is when a trader makes a new high in their trading accounts. Sometimes if you go on a losing streak with large losers, your account will go for a long time without hitting a new high. The longer the drawdown, the harder it is to come back.

  In fact if you lose 50% of your account value, you need to make 100% just to get back to breakeven—this is extremely hard to do. It also is emotionally damaging to your trading psychology.

  Figure 11.1 shows how hard it is to come back from a drawdown.

  I have some hard rules to help me keep my drawdowns low. My goal is to never have them go over 5% so I can always come back from my losses quickly with less stress.

Drawdown-stopping rules

1. Stop trading if you lose three trades in a row.

   If I hit a three-trade losing streak, I am done for the day. This is not always easy, and when it happens, I continue to want to trade, but I do this so that I can make sure I come back the next day.

2. My maximum loss for any day is 1.5%.

   This is similar to rule 1. If I am down 1.5%, I can bounce back with one or two winning days. But if my losses are any larger, it gets much harder.

Loss of capital (%)	Gain to recover (%)
5	5.3
10	11.1
15	17.6
20	25.0
25	33.3
30	42.9
35	53.8
40	66.7
45	81.8
50	100.0
55	122.0
60	150.0

Figure 11.1   The Bigger the Drawdown the Harder It Is to Recover
SOURCE: https://www.turtletrader.com/recovery/.

I recently interviewed Blake Morrow from Forex Analytix, and he said that if you are digging yourself into a hole, the first thing you need to do is stop digging.[1]

This is the reason I have these two rules and follow them no matter what. Some people dig so deep they dig their own graves. I don't want to do that!

3. Stop trading for the week if you have two losing days in a row.

This is a hard rule that I follow because if I have two losing days at 1.5% each, that is a 3% drawdown, and that is the limit of what I want to hit as far as equity drawdown. Taking a break for the rest of the week helps to get your mind relaxed and ready to trade again the next week. Protect that drawdown at all costs.

4. Stop when I am ahead.

If I have a good day, one thing that I try to never do is to give back the money. It is mentally damaging when you have good profit and keep trading and you give some or all of the profit back. When I have a good day, I book my profits and take the rest of the day off.

Small Gains Add Up Over Time

You do not have to make money every day, and you do not have to make money every week or even every month. If you can continually make a small amount over a long period of time, you will be extremely successful over the long term.

If you can make 1% profit per month compounded, that will give you a yearly profit of 12.68% per year. This may not seem like a lot but it is the secret to creating great wealth.

If you start with a $50,000 balance, 1% is $500, which doesn't seem like a lot on its own, but that will grow over time and at the end of the first year you will earn $6,341, which is a great ROI!

In fact if you continue at this conservative pace over the course of 20 years, you will earn $494,627.68 (see Figures 11.2 and 11.3).

This is the power of big-picture thinking versus getting caught up with just one loss. On a $50,000 account, 1% is just $500, and you can earn $500 by taking just one trade.

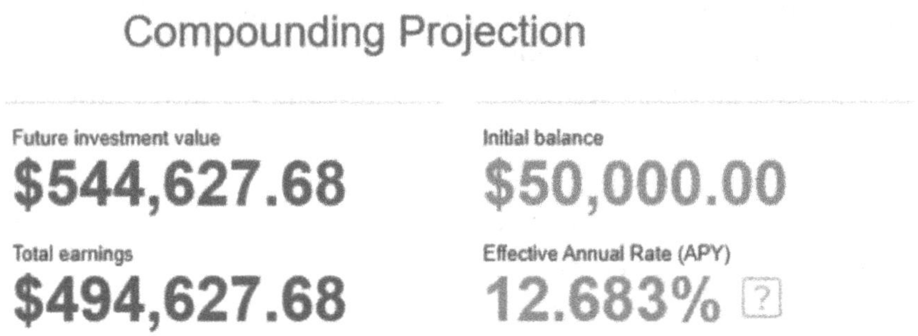

Compounding Projection

Future investment value
$544,627.68

Initial balance
$50,000.00

Total earnings
$494,627.68

Effective Annual Rate (APY)
12.683% [?]

Figure 11.2   Small Gains Over Time Equal Large Returns
SOURCE: https://www.thecalculatorsite.com/finance/calculators/forex-compound-calculator.php.

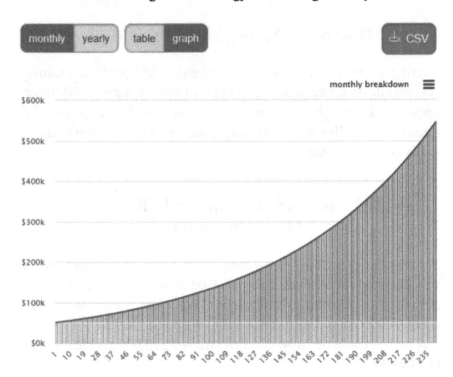

Figure 11.3   1% Gain per Month for 20 Years
SOURCE: https://www.thecalculatorsite.com/finance/calculators/
forex-compound-calculator.php.

You could literally trade just once a month and earn half a million dollars by working one day a month. It is amazing to think about the potential free time you could have if you took just one trade a month and spent the rest of the time doing your normal day-to-day activities.

The idea that you can earn a sizeable amount of revenue by only trading one day a month enlightens the fact that you do not have to be glued to the computer screens all the time to be a successful trader.

How Much Money Should You Risk?

There is no correct answer to the question of how much money you should risk because it depends on your personal risk tolerance, but I strongly recommend considering the recommendations I gave earlier about keeping drawdown low so that you can easily come back from the losses.

Risk Examples to Help You Build a Risk Management Plan

Position sizing is how big a position you will open. If you have a $50,000 account and you open a $10,000 position of a stock, that is ⅕ of your account at risk. Now if you close the trade when it is down $500 dollars, that is a 1% loss on your account, but a 5% loss on the trade because you only traded $10,000 and $500 is 5% of $10,000.

When you have multiple positions open at one time, you must calculate total account risk. If you have 20 trades open, you might think that there is no way you can lose them all because you are diversified. However, in the stock market positions will often move in the same direction when the market is having a down day, so (if each one of those 20 trades risks 1%) you could easily lose 20% in a single day.

The way to avoid this is to limit the number of open positions you have at one time.

Winning Larger Trades Than You Lose

Figure 11.4 is a risk-to-reward chart that I display on my site TradingStrategyGuides.com. I use this to help traders understand how important it is to manage their risk to reward.

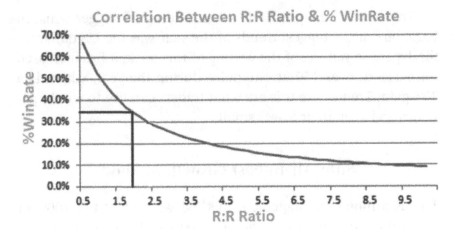

Figure 11.4   Winning Percentage Needed versus Trade Size to Be Profitable
SOURCE: TradingStrategyGuides.com.

If you lose $1 on a trade and then make $10 on another trade, you can make money by being right only 10% of the time. The smaller the risk-to-reward ratio, the higher the win rate you need to be profitable. This is a balance that traders must learn to master to always be working at increasing profits.

If you can learn the discipline of finding the big winning trades, you can be a successful trader. This might seem like a lot, but there are stocks that continue to double in value many times over.

When a stock increases by 10 times 900% it is called a *10 bagger*. To get these types of results takes time and long-term holding, but the strategy of getting trades like this, and then compounding the wins over and over again, will allow a trader to grow their accounts quickly.

Nicolas Darvas, in his book *How I Made $2,000,000 in the Stock Market*, used a strategy of holding on to his winners as long as he could to grow his account. This strategy allowed trades to continue on in the direction of the trend.

Trends can be a great tool when trading for bigger wins. In 2022, one of the biggest trends of the year was the US dollar vs. the Japanese yen. As of the writing of this book, it has increased from 115 to over 150 at one point during the year, which is a 30% gain. Trends like this are what traders can use to win larger trades and keep their losses small.

Safe All-In Fast Growth Method

This is a money management method where you use 100% of your capital on each trade and only take one trade at a time.

Here is how it works: with a $50,000 portfolio you can buy shares with the entire $50,000 balance, which means if you buy a stock that is $100, you can purchase 500 shares. The way you calculate how many shares you can buy is to divide the share price ($100) by $50,000, which is the amount of capital in your trading account.

When you buy those 100 shares, it is wise to keep the risk low, somewhere between 1% to 5% because this is your entire account at risk. The last thing you want to do is not have a stop loss, because if you don't, the price can go down and you will be holding on to a losing trade for months or years, and that is not a great way to grow your account consistently.

It is possible to get a 10%, 20%, 100%, or even 1000% return on a single trade. The key is to ride the trend.

Figure 11.5 shows a Domino's Pizza trade example. You would want to put the stop loss below that key support level, around the 102 price point. If you hit the stop loss of your 500 shares, then you will lose 1% of your total account value, which is only $500.

You can see the profit potential on a trade like this because Domino's ended up getting to $200 per share, so in this example it is possible to make $50,000 on a single trade.

Figure 11.5   Domino's Pizza Bullish Trade Entry
SOURCE: TrendSpider.

Going all-in on one trade, also known as "concentrating your bets," can have several advantages, despite the conventional wisdom that diversification is key to reducing risk. Here are some advantages of going all-in:

- **Increased focus:** By putting all of your efforts into one trade, you can focus all of your attention on making that trade a success. This increased focus can lead to better research, which can make for a larger profit.
- **Potential for higher returns:** If the trade is successful, concentrating your bets can lead to higher returns compared to a more diversified portfolio. This is because the success of the one trade has a larger impact on the overall portfolio.
- **Better understanding:** By focusing on one trade, you can gain a deeper understanding of the market, the trade involved, and the risks associated with the trade. This deeper understanding can help you make better decisions and potentially improve your chances of growing your account quickly.

However, it's important to note that this method might potentially be riskier, as putting all of your resources into one trade leaves you open to one big loss.

To control this risk, it's important to have a solid understanding of the trade and to know when to get out of the trade. It's important to monitor the trade and have an exit strategy in place in case the trade starts to move against you.

Stock Trade Management Plan for a $50,000 Account

Another approach to money management with a $50,000 account would be making 10 trades at a time instead of 1 trade at a time as discussed in the previous section. This would be $5,000 of shares purchased per trade. With each of those, we would risk 1% on the trade, which would only be $50. If you have 10 trades open at one time, that would be a total risk of 10% of the account at one time.

If you didn't want to spread it around as much, you could do five trades at a time and risk 2%, and that would still be a max risk of 10%.

Forex Trading Risk Management

When trading the Forex, market risk is a little bit different. Forex trading is done on margin, and you buy what are known as "lots." One lot is $100,000 of currency-buying power.

The price increments are calculated in pips, not cents. "Pip" means Percentage in Point. That is a smaller unit of measurement than a penny. Most currency pairs have four or five decimal points, and the pip is the 4th decimal. When price moves .0001 to .0002, that is a one-pip move. It is 1/100 of 1 percent. On most currency pairs, the value of one lot is .10 cents per pip.

Risk Calculations for Forex

Each currency pair has a different calculation for how much the $100,000 lot size gains per pip. Most pairs are $10 per pip per lot. If you are trading 10 lots, it would be $100 per pip.

If you have a $50,000 account and you are trading one lot, your stop loss would need to be 50 pips to risk 1% on the trade. The way to calculate risk is to take the risk per pip and multiply that by the number of pips. In this case, 50 * 10 = $500, which is a 1% risk on the total account value.

Riding the trends for Forex trading can give you profitable trades. Figure 11.6 shows a recent trade on the USDJPY.

In this example, if we ride this trend with one lot that is $10 per pip and it went $4,000 pips, that would be a $40,000 trade.

Risk management is such an important part of trading successfully. This was the most difficult thing for me to master in my own trading, and over the many years I have been teaching traders this is the hardest thing for them to learn. The concepts are simple, but the discipline required is the hard part. That is

Figure 11.6   Massive Trend Trade with Very Good Risk Management
SOURCE: TrendSpider.

why this book started out with a teaching mindset. We must have the proper mindset and discipline to practice proper risk management.

Learn these techniques and practice them, and apply them to your trading, and you will never have to worry about being a losing trader. Trading is about risk management and probabilities.

Summary

In this chapter, we discussed the importance of risk management in trading. Several key principles were emphasized, including:

- **Keeping losses small:** Limiting losses by setting stop-loss orders and controlling the size of trades relative to the size of the investment portfolio is important in avoiding the potential for large losses.
- **Letting winners ride:** By letting winning trades run, traders can potentially capture more of the upside potential of a winning trade.
- **1% per month equals massive gains:** Consistent returns of just 1% per month can lead to significant gains over time. By effectively managing risk, traders can aim to achieve consistent, small gains each month.

This chapter hammered home the crucial role of risk management in trading and discussed several key principles for effectively managing risk.

By keeping losses small, letting winners ride, and aiming for consistent small gains, traders can improve the overall performance of their trading and minimize the potential for losses.

Note

1. https://podcast.tradingstrategyguides.com/currencies-trading-with-pip-czar-blake-morrow-ep-136/.

Chapter 12

Creating a Road Map
for Massive Success

A journey of a thousand miles begins with a single step.
– Chinese proverb

rading can be exciting and rewarding, but it can also be challenging and frustrating. With so many variables at play, it's easy to feel overwhelmed and unsure of where to start. That's why it's crucial to have a plan in place, a road map that guides you toward your desired outcomes.

In this chapter, we'll be discussing the importance of having a vision, creating a trading plan, setting small goals and milestones, and regularly reviewing your progress. With a clear roadmap in place, you'll have a guide that helps you stay focused and motivated, even when the markets are volatile. We'll provide you with the tools you need to make informed decisions, maximize your potential, and achieve massive success in your trading journey. So buckle up and let's get started!

Life is a journey, and I have had some great experiences along the way. They are all amazing. The massive upward climbs and the downward spirals. The amazing wins and the agonizing losses. The journey is what makes life great.

Trading is a journey and when we go on a trip we need to make a plan for that trip. I personally am kind of a wild and crazy guy. On many trips I ended up sleeping on a bench in a bus station or in the city square.

Now that I am older I don't do that anymore. If we move forward like that in trading, we go broke, and we go broke fast. In fact, that is how I began my trading career. I wanted to make money and make money fast, and I found out that things don't work that way in trading. To accomplish things in life and in trading, you need to have a plan.

There are three major steps for getting a road map for success. Those steps are creating a vision, getting a plan, and reviewing that plan and vision on a regular basis.

A Big Vision for Trading

Simon Sinek famously said that we must first start with the question *why*.[1]

This is a critical part of setting up a big vision for trading success.

Why do you want to trade?

It is a simple question, but we need to answer it, and then we need to focus on that each and every day. Because if we do not know in our heart of hearts why we want to do something, we will give up along the way.

You might be thinking about making money. Yes, making money is why we all enter trading. But *why* do you want to make money?

There are potentially a million reasons why you want to make money and what you will do with your money. It could be that you want to leave an inheritance for your children and grandchildren. Possibly because you want to have the freedom to travel.

Successful people know what they want, and they know why they want it.

I live in Pennsylvania, and I am from Oregon. When I got married and had kids I made it a priority to visit parents and grandparents every year because family is important to me. Every summer for the past 17 years, I have gotten my family into a minivan, and we make the journey 2,500 miles across this nation from Pennsylvania to Oregon.

It usually takes four or five days to get there. We stay there for about two or three weeks, and it takes us four or five days to drive back. That is a vacation of four or five weeks in length each year.

It is a fantastic blessing to be able to do this. I am so grateful and do not take it for granted. I realize that many people do not have the luxury to do this type of beautiful family traveling.

This is possible because I am a trader and business owner. I can continue to make money wherever I am located in the world because of trading, and I have people who work for me who can continue to earn revenue for me while I am away.

But it was actually made possible because I first had a vision to go on those trips; it was important to me, and I made it a priority to figure out how I was going to make it happen.

This is why you must have a vision for your trading and for your life if you want to accomplish your goals.

Take a moment to think about why you want to trade.

Is it to create a revenue stream on the side? Perhaps you are retired and need something to spend your time on. Maybe you want to trade full time for a living so you can leave your job. Maybe it is to create an inheritance to leave to your grandchildren. Maybe you want to become a prop firm trader.

I believe knowing the answer to this question is a critical catapult for success for traders.

Grab a notebook and pen or pencil and start writing out your vision. For detailed information about writing a vision, I recommend two books that helped me. One is *Living Forward* by Michael Hyatt, and the other is *Vivid Vision* by Cameron Herold. Both of those books have helped me tremendously in planning and articulating my vision.

Create a Plan for Trading Mastery

Now that you have your vision and you know why you want to trade, you need a plan. This chapter is a guide to help you. I titled this chapter "Creating a Road Map for Massive Success," because a road map is a plan—a path—for you to follow to keep you on track.

One of the problems of a big vision is it can be so big that it can be hard to transform into reality. One of my mentors, Pastor Keith Tucci, often says a vision without a plan is a fantasy.

You must have a plan to follow, or else your vision is just a big dream that will never happen.

In September 2020 I went on a 70-mile hike in the Laurel Highlands State Park in Pennsylvania. For this journey, there were many things I had to do to be successful.

- I had to plan a training regimen to make sure my body was strong enough to complete the journey.
- I had to plan for the equipment that I would need for the trip.
- I had to plan and gather the food and water I would need for the trip.
- I had to get a map and plan for where I was going to take shelter and plan on how far I was going to travel each day.
- I had to get a map and become familiar with the route so I would know where I was going.

Putting this together I had a big vision of completing a 70-mile trip because I wanted to experience nature and test my hiking skills. Then I had to come up with a plan.

In the same way I put together a plan for hiking, we need to put together a plan for our trading. Ask yourself the following questions:

- What are my big-picture goals?
- What type of trading do I need to do to accomplish those goals?
- When am I going to trade?
- What is my trading strategy?
- What are my risk parameters?
- How much capital will I need?
- How will I continue to motivate myself to keep moving forward?
- How will I measure success or forward growth?

These are the basic questions you can start asking to help yourself come up with a plan to become a successful trader.

Once you have your big vision and your plan in place, you need to have an execution plan.

Small Goals and Mile Markers

A big vision is big and scary. It is overwhelming at times, and it can seem impossible. That's why I break it down into bite-size pieces.

If your goal is to become a millionaire trader and you only have $500 in your trading account, you need to understand that this is going to be a journey that will have many ups and downs along the way.

Before you make $1 million you need to make $1.

Make a mile marker.

The Laurel Highlands trail that I hiked has mile markers along the way. Every mile there is a stone pillar that lets you know you've made an additional mile.

My big goal was to hike 70 miles. My small goal was to make it one mile. Whenever I was on that trail and I saw that mile marker, I felt a bit of joy, hope, and relief. I was like "One mile down, only 69 miles to go! Yes I can do this!"

In trading we could say I made $1, now I only have $999,999 to go! Yes I can do this!

I was always looking for that next mile marker on the trail. I knew that I was always close, and every time I hit one it was great.

Having smaller goals makes the journey manageable and more realistic. The old saying "How do you eat an elephant? One bite at a time" is true. We need to take things one step at a time.

I have been teaching traders for many years, and I tell people to start small. I get a lot of pushback for that. One person recently told me, "I'm not wasting my time trading for peanuts." That person didn't have a vision and did not understand that successful trading is a process. We start small, and we grow and we accomplish our massive goals by taking one step at a time.

Seriously, you need to learn how to make $1 before you can make $1 million.

Another thing that is important with small achievable subgoals to help you accomplish your larger goal is that it helps us measure where we are in the big picture of our main goal.

When I was on that 70-mile trail and I saw the 35-mile marker, I knew I was halfway there. This is such a great moment. It is a time to celebrate! Yes, I haven't accomplished my task yet, but I had just walked 35 miles. It was a big deal to me at the time.

We must measure where we are along the path. My journey as a successful trader took much longer for success than it needed to, and one of the reasons was because I didn't have a plan and I did not have clear smaller goals along the way. Because of this, there were many times when I almost quit because of discouragement.

The reason trading has such a high failure rate is because people quit before they have accomplished their goals, and they quit because they get discouraged. If you are making small steps forward, that is not discouraging. It is a great deal of motivation to keep moving forward.

Having smaller reachable mini-goals along the way gives us a renewed focus and energy to give us what we need to finish the course.

The last thing that having smaller mini-goals or mile markers does for traders is let you know when you are off course. There were several times in my 70-mile hike that I accidentally got off the trail. During those times, because I was off the trail, those miles did not count toward the destination. I probably hiked about 75 miles, but the trail was only 70.

If you get off course and never get back on, then you will never accomplish the goal. This is another reason why traders quit when they get off course and don't even realize it. This is all because they did not have a set of clear measurable actions that they can take to accomplish their goals.

Don't be a statistic. Make a plan with clear goals along the way. Each step you take gets you one step closer. You can do this!

Measuring your progress to make sure you are on track is important. It is always a balancing act—keeping your eye on the big vision and the short-term goals. When walking down the road, I keep my head up looking at the horizon to where I want to go, but I also look down often to make sure I'm not stepping off a cliff. I have to keep both big picture and short term in my focus at all times.

Schedule Review Periods on a Regular Basis

Here are some things you can add to your plan to help you stay on track.

- Daily goals
- Weekly goals
- Monthly goals
- Yearly goals
- Revenue goals
- Execution and mindset goals

It is important to schedule times for review sessions because, if you are anything like me, you are a busy person, and if you don't schedule it, it will not happen.

I am always reviewing my goals on a daily, weekly, monthly, and yearly basis. I put the time on my calendar, and I get out my notebook, and I get to work.

It doesn't take long to do the reviews, but it is critical to keeping me calibrated and on track, moving forward to my destination.

Summary

In this chapter you learned about how to create a roadmap by crafting your big vision, creating a plan you can follow with small goals and a scheduled review process. If you take this process seriously and do the steps that are in this book, you will be a successful trader.

We discussed the importance of having a vision and a plan in place when it comes to trading. We emphasized the need to create a trading plan that outlines your goals and strategies, as well as setting small goals and milestones along the way to help you stay motivated and focused.

Additionally, we emphasized the importance of regularly reviewing your progress to ensure that you are on track toward your desired outcomes.

By having a clear roadmap in place, you'll be able to make informed decisions, avoid common pitfalls, and maximize your potential for success.

Overall, this chapter provides a comprehensive guide to help traders create a roadmap for massive success in the world of trading.

Note

1. https://simonsinek.com/books/start-with-why/.

Part IV

Maximizing Profits

Welcome to the final part of the Complete Trading System. In Chapter 13, you will discover the powerful strategy that I have developed over 25 years of investing and trading. This strategy is designed to maximize your trading profits and help you become a successful investor. By the end of this chapter, you will have finished the book, and you will have a clear understanding of how to apply this strategy to your own trading and achieve consistent profits in the markets. So, buckle up and get ready to take your trading to the next level!

Chapter 13

Profit-Maximizing Strategy

Investing and trading can be an exciting and potentially lucrative endeavor, but it also comes with its own set of challenges.

As we all know, inflation is a constant threat to our wealth, and it can be tempting to trade our time for money in order to keep pace. However, in this chapter, we'll explore a different approach to maximizing profits in the world of trading.

We'll take a look at my own journey as an investor and how I got started on this path. Additionally, we'll delve into the power of investing in trading strategies, new technologies, and companies with great leaders. We'll also discuss the benefits of using the power of dollar cost averaging to maximize your profits over time. This chapter is all about using your money to make money. This is the best way to grow your wealth.

I stumbled on investing when I was extremely young, and I was fortunate for that. It has been a source of income for me for my entire life, and I am going to share my strategy and the backstory of how I was able to learn and optimize my strategy of making money in the market.

This strategy I have learned over the past 26 years will show you how to:

- Invest in the best stocks
- Find fast growth opportunities
- Create money in your sleep
- Keep drawdowns low

In this chapter I am going to share how I have been able to generate a steady stream of income through investing and not trading. By the end of this chapter, you'll have a better understanding of how to maximize your profits and build long-term wealth through smart and strategic investing. So let's get started!

Beginnings

When I first started trading back in 1996 I had very little money. I was going to Portland Community College and didn't have any income coming in. I realized quickly that college wasn't for me. I hated school. There was no purpose in it for me. One day I ran into an Army recruiter in the hallway and it didn't take much for him to mention the adventure that I could have, so I quit school and joined the Army, which for me was a fantastic decision. I received orders to go to Germany as part of the 1st infantry division.

In 1996 when I joined the Army—which was the first job I ever had—I made $800 a month, which isn't a substantial amount. After taxes it ended up being about $150 a week of free cash flow. However, the Army did pay for my housing, food, utilities, and medical benefits. This meant that the $150 a week was 100% my money to do with whatever I wanted.

My dad worked hard as a diesel mechanic, and my mom was at home raising us, doing the cooking, and taking care of the house. Since my parents had four kids, the paycheck of one mechanic didn't go very far. The hard work ethic and frugal background I learned from my parents was the perfect ingredient to help me get ahead in life.

I wanted to get out of being in financial trouble, and I made a plan as a very young 19-year-old with not much experience in the world. The first part of the plan was to save. I had never had any money before, but I saved everything that I made from the Army. I always ate the free food, and I didn't spend much on extras. I was able to save up my money fast.

It was odd to me because my friends in the Army were living paycheck to paycheck and yet I was building quite a nest egg because I was saving most of what I made.

My friends actually felt bad for me because I didn't have any extra items in my room. It was just bare. They would stop by and donate comfortable comforters since I used the green wool scratchy blanket the Army gave me for my bed. They would give me clothing because I only had two changes of civilian clothes. I told them: "Hey, I'm not broke. I just don't want to spend the money." But they insisted on giving me stuff. The good friends I had were always looking out for me.

After doing this, I realized I needed to find a way to create more money from my savings that I was developing.

It was at this time that I remembered the stock-trading lessons I learned from my dad. I decided to open a stock-trading account. I opened my first brokerage account in 1997 with E-Trade. By the time I left Germany at the beginning of the year 2000 I had a nest egg valued at over $30,000. As shown in Figure 13.1, adjusted for inflation, in today's money that would be a total of $51,918. Not bad since I was only making $800 a month.

Most of the examples I give in this chapter are from memory, so they are estimates, not exact calculations, but they are close. What's important are the lessons I learned, not the exact figures.

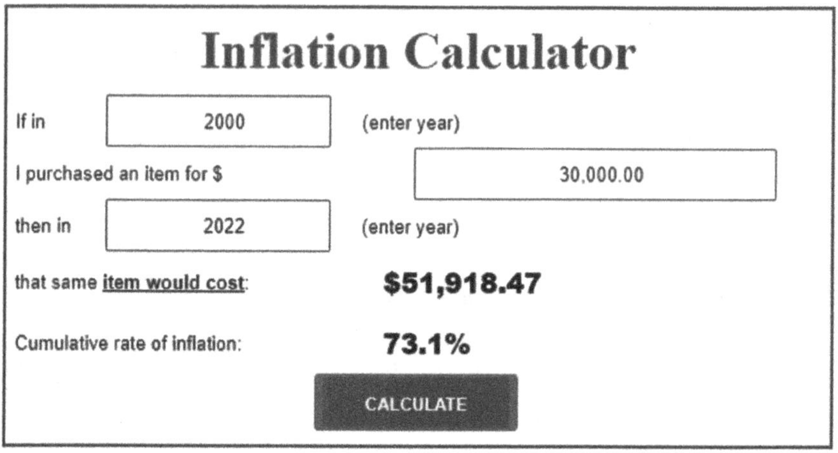

Inflation Calculator

If in	2000	(enter year)
I purchased an item for $		30,000.00
then in	2022	(enter year)
that same item would cost:	**$51,918.47**	
Cumulative rate of inflation:	**73.1%**	

CALCULATE

Figure 13.1   The Value of Your Money Gets Less
SOURCE: https://www.usinflationcalculator.com/.

Inflation refers to the sustained increase in the general price level of goods and services in an economy over a period of time. It is influenced by many factors, including the money supply. When there is an increase in the money supply, there is more money in circulation chasing the same amount of goods and services, which can result in higher prices. The central bank has two major tools to control inflation: interest rates and the creation of new money. By adjusting interest rates, the central bank can affect the cost of borrowing and the demand for goods and services. By controlling the creation of new money, the central bank can directly influence the money supply and ultimately inflation.

I had to decide what stocks I was going to purchase, but I didn't have any education in stock trading other than a few things I had learned from my dad. I started out by picking only four companies, and I decided on those from experience I had with them.

- Intel: My aunt Mary worked for Intel, and I loved computers, so I decided to start weekly buying Intel stock. This worked out; from roughly $19.72 per share around the time I started the value grew to $70 per share for a sweet little profit of 254% return on investment (see Figure 13.2).

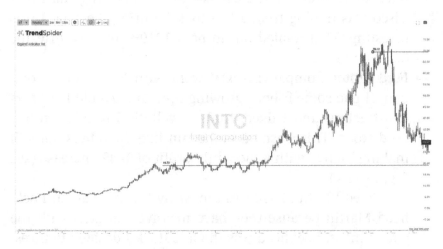

Figure 13.2 Price of Intel in the Late 1990s
SOURCE: TrendSpider.

Figure 13.3   CSCO in the Late 1990s
SOURCE: TrendSpider.

- Cisco: Before I dropped out of college, I was going to be a network administrator, so I learned about Cisco Network software and decided to invest in Cisco. I guess college wasn't a total waste after all. You can see in the following chart that Cisco was trading from $5.94 to $78 during the time I was investing. That totaled out to be a 1219% increase in value (see Figure 13.3).
- Ford Motor Company: Next I went with Ford Motor Company. I had some friends growing up that liked old Ford cars and tractors, and I liked Ford as well. So I decided to buy Ford stock. This wasn't a home run like the others but still making money with a nice little profit of 144% increase (see Figure 13.4).
- Lockheed Martin: Lastly, in the Army I learned about Lockheed Martin because they have massive contracts with the government. Lockheed was the last stock I decided to invest in at that time. This one didn't work out as well because I ended up with a loss of 28% on that one (see Figure 13.5).

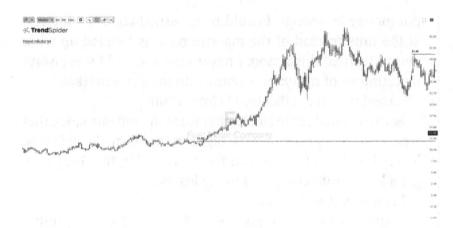

Figure 13.4   Ford Motor Company in the Late 1990s
SOURCE: TrendSpider.

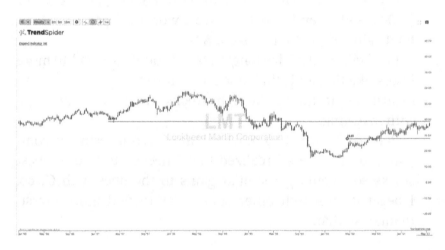

Figure 13.5   Lockheed Martin in the Late 1990s
SOURCE: TrendSpider.

This was a great start for me because I learned many valuable lessons that I still use every day in my life.

- I learned that I could make money on autopilot.

    By investing in the market and working my job I could continue to make money on my investments. If I had just put money in savings, I could have earned about 1% interest at the time instead of the massive returns I ended up with. Once I learned this lesson, I never forgot it, and I was always investing all of my extra revenue into the stock market.

• I learned that diversification is important.

Because I had three stocks that went up and one stock that went down, I learned that the bigger winners made up for the losses I took. In fact my winners were so big that they gave me a huge profit compared to my losers.

Let me explain further.

I purchased CSCO originally for $5.94, and with my initial investment of $1,000 I was able to get 168 shares. By the time I sold, that was a profit of $10,784 on the initial investment.

My only loss was LMT. I initially bought 25 shares for $1,000, and when I sold, those were worth $25 per share for a total value of $725 for a loss of $275.

I will take that all day long! In fact, I could have had 10 more losers like that and still made a nice profit.

• I learned that finding the right stocks was a huge advantage with investing.

Because I earned so much on my Cisco investment compared to the others I realized that I needed to find the best stocks so I could get similar gains to the ones with Cisco. I began to research other companies to find more investments like that.

Trading Time for Money

An important concept in business is trading time for money. That means you work a job and you get paid for your time. When I was investing in the market while working in the Army I was trading time for money, on autopilot.

Most people never get ahead because time is limited and we can only earn a limited amount of money. Time is our most valuable resource, and smart businesspeople and traders learn to earn revenue without having to spend time to earn money.

When working a traditional job, it is important to find another stream of revenue where you can put your money to work and have it earn revenue for you without taking your time to do so.

Trading is a great way to earn revenue because you can scale it and grow it to large amounts of money. Profitable and successful traders can earn a great living, up to millions of dollars. However, the drawback is that they still have to work for their money and are trading time for money.

An additional strategy helps us to earn additional revenue from our trading profits by taking some of the money we make from trading and *investing* it. This is how we begin to build real wealth, and ultimately we will not have to trade time for money any longer.

I have a strategy to take the money I earn from trading to invest it into the markets.

Investing Trading Strategy

When you buy a stock you become a part owner of the company you own shares in. Most people earn real wealth through businesses. People that own businesses are ones that make great money because the business becomes a vehicle to create wealth.

This stock-picking strategy I have created helps to find massive gains using companies that continue to grow. I am going to explain how to find stocks to trade that can give a massive return on investment.

There are three steps to finding great companies to invest in that I am going to be going to go over in detail:

1. Invest in new technology
2. Invest in good company leadership
3. Choose the top companies in their field

Those three things will give you a massive edge in learning how to invest for success.

Invest in New Technology

Over the past 120 years, most of the wealth-creating stocks were companies that created innovation and changed the world with their businesses. These world-changing technologies come from people like John D. Rockefeller with Standard Oil, Andrew Carnegie with Carnegie Steel, and Henry Ford of Ford Motor Company. Or the invention of harnessing electricity and the telephone to help keep us comfortable and enable communication. These inventions improve life and create wealth.

These were new companies with new technology that made the lives of people better. Oil was helpful because people used it to light their homes, heat their homes, and then used it to power their vehicles. This energy discovery was a massive improvement to the quality of life for the entire planet. We also have companies like McDonald's, which made it more convenient to eat quickly, and it made our lives more convenient.

Recently, companies like Apple with computers, AOL with the internet, Microsoft with software, and Intel with microprocessors have been among the foremost innovators. Amazon has made our lives better by giving us access to shopping with the click of a button. The stock prices of all these companies have grown so fast that not just the owners have gotten rich but also those who invest in those companies. Bill Gates, the founder of Microsoft, was the richest man in the world at 31 years old in 1987 and Mark Zuckerberg, the founder of Facebook, at 23.[1]

A *Washington Post* article from 2003 claims that over 8,000 Microsoft employees retired early as millionaires.[2]

What all of these companies had in common is that they were pioneers in their fields and changed the world. We just have to find the next pioneers.

Then we can also take advantage of that and also retire early.

Invest in Leadership

Ideas are amazing, and they change the world, but an idea will only go so far. To have a massive impact that creates massive wealth that idea must be connected to a visionary leader. These leaders have the ambition and drive to carry those ideas out. People who are visionary and combine that with strong leadership skills are the people that I like to invest in.

Find a company with a strong leader—we know that those people defy the odds time and again, and they will not quit when times get difficult.

People like Bill Gates, Phil Knight, Jeff Bezos, Andrew Carnegie, Henry Ford, John D. Rockefeller, Elon Musk, and Mark Zuckerberg are passionate leaders and visionaries who have created companies, technology, and wealth that people who are paying attention can get on board with and invest in.

I do not invest in any company that does not have visionary leaders. We have an advantage because now with social media and the internet we can watch videos, listen to podcasts, and learn about these leaders. Don't just learn from them, invest in them.

Invest in the Top of the Field

It's good to focus on the best of the best.

Leaders have power in shaping and influencing their respective fields. Whether it be in business, sports, science, or music, there are always people who stand out and achieve much more than the average person.

These leaders possess qualities, such as vision, drive, and determination. These qualities allow them to achieve success and ultimately change the world. In the business world, leaders like Jeff Bezos, Elon Musk, and Warren Buffett are great examples of this. They have demonstrated the ability to create and grow successful companies, revolutionize industries, and generate wealth for themselves and their shareholders. They have a clear vision for the future and the drive to make it happen. If you invest in them, they take their companies to new heights.

In sports, leaders like LeBron James, Serena Williams, and Lionel Messi are known for greatness. They have set records, won numerous championships, and inspired millions of fans around the world with their performances.

The key here is to focus on great leaders.

A principle discovered by mathematician Vilfredo Pareto, born in 1848, is now called the "Pareto Principle." According to Wikipedia, "Pareto noticed that approximately 80% of Italy's land was owned by 20% of the population."[3]

What has been further discovered is that this applies to many parts of the economy as well. For example, the top 20% of employees will deliver 80% of the results. The top 20% of your products in business will generate 80% of the sales.

This principle is used to help scale businesses. For example, if you know that the top 20% of your products produce 80%, cut out all the products except the very best. That way all your effort is going toward those things that are producing results.

If you cut the poor-performing employees, you can eliminate lots of poor productivity, which can then cause rapid growth.

This same principle can be applied to trading.

Look at your trades—you will see that you have several big trades, which account for the majority of your profits, and you will see some big losers that account for the majority of your losses. Analyze each specific type of trade, then avoid the big losers and even avoid the small losers. Focus on only the big winners, and you will have a formula for successful trading.

Remember, only 20% of the people you are trading against will be willing to do this extra work. When *you* do that extra work, it gives you an edge to be successful.

When a new idea or new technology comes into the market, there are usually many companies that jump into the arena. How do you know which ones to invest in?

Invest in the best of the group. There will always be one company or individual that will rise above the pack. This is the company that we want to be investing in.

If we pick the wrong company, no big deal, just sell your shares and invest in the best later on. There is no reason to be afraid of losing because we all pick the wrong ones at times; just close it and pick something better next time.

Right now we have many investing opportunities. We have new technologies moving faster than ever before, and these will create opportunities like we have never seen before.

Here are some things that I am looking at right now. We have new auto technology with self-driving cars and electric vehicles. We have new things happening in the gaming industry with the metaverse and other gaming technologies. There is new technology coming in the fields of medicine and science as well. In medicine new discoveries and opportunities are happening every day.

There is a new money system with Bitcoin and crypto. It is still early to get involved in these fields. Do your research, find the leaders, and invest in them.

The Power of Dollar Cost Averaging

One of the things that has helped me develop tremendous gains with investing is *dollar cost averaging*. This means that you put in a fixed dollar amount on a regular basis. I started doing this by investing every week when I was 19 years old, and I continue to do it to this day. If the stock goes up, I buy shares. If it goes down, I buy shares. If we do this over time in the companies we believe in, even if they go down, we will see amazing gains over a period of time.

I am going to give some examples of how this works, and I thought I would blow your mind with the first example.

If you had put $100 a week in Bitcoin starting in 2010, now you would have $217,057,416.05—not bad for $100 a week! (See Figure 13.6.)

This just shows that you don't need a lot of money to become wealthy.

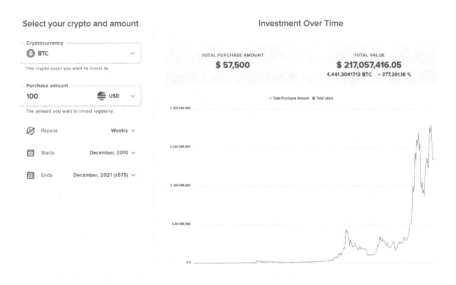

Figure 13.6 Dollar Cost Averaging Bitcoin

SOURCE: https://uphold.com/en-us/get-started/dollar-cost-averaging-calculator.

Don't Stop Investing

My biggest failure is that I have had several periods in my life where I stopped the gains. The first time was in 2000 when I closed all my trades and invested the profits in a carpet cleaning business. I ended up losing all that investment. It was a good idea that just didn't work out. I have had several places in my life when I took the money out. When I look back, if I had stuck it out, I would be worth at least $300,000 million. Good thing I can look back and laugh.

I share that here because no matter how old you are it's not too late to start again, and if you are younger and reading this, you have a great opportunity to start investing now and invest in the right things.

The great thing about being a trader is that we can earn a lot of revenue, and if we use the revenue from our trading to invest, we can add quite a bit of dollar cost averaging and grow our nest eggs much faster than with many other jobs. That is, if we are a profitable trader.

Here is a summary of the formula that you need to execute to be successful.

- New technology or company.
- Visionary leader.
- Invest in the leader.
- Start small and keep investing.
- Consistency—don't stop.

This is a simple strategy that works. I know many traders who, if they would just implement that one strategy, would be extremely well off, but they wanted to get rich quick trading and instead blew trading account after trading account. If you are struggling with trading, please consider switching to the investing strategy.

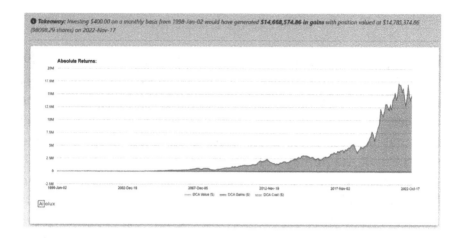

Figure 13.7 Dollar Cost Averaging Apple
SOURCE: aiolux.com.

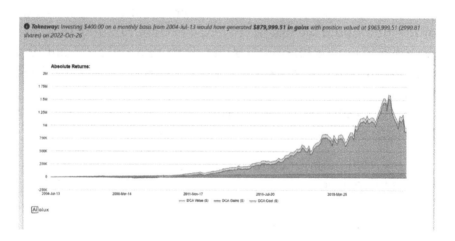

Figure 13.8 Dollar Cost Averaging Domino's Pizza
SOURCE: aiolux.com.

The following figures show examples of dollar cost averaging success. Figure 13.7 shows Apple at $400 a month.

Figure 13.8 shows Dominos Pizza.

Figure 13.9 shows Tesla.

Figure 13.10 shows McDonald's.

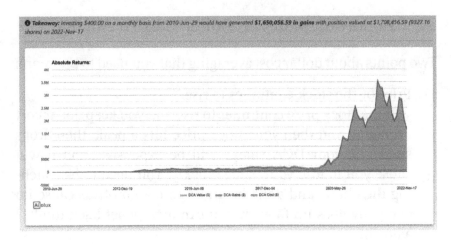

Figure 13.9 Dollar Cost Averaging Tesla
SOURCE: `aiolux.com`.

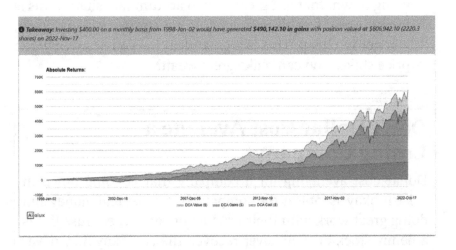

Figure 13.10 Dollar Cost Averaging McDonald's
SOURCE: `aiolux.com`.

Important Notes on Dollar Cost Averaging

Two points about dollar cost averaging that you need to know are:

1. Price of the stock continues to rise.

   If the stock price continues to rise and you keep dollar cost averaging and then your stock price hits a peak, then drops suddenly, your DCA shares will be expensive, and it will cause you to lose your value quickly. You need to be watching the charts and don't be afraid to take profit because no company goes up forever. You can always get back in after a downturn.

2. Dollar cost averaging a major loser.

   If you continue to dollar cost average when the price is going down, that is a great way to accumulate shares; this is how the real wealth is created. If your price is going down, you get in cheap. This is a great deal for you because when price spikes you can make great wealth.

Don't Dollar Cost Average a Losing Company

Dollar cost averaging for a company that is going down in price is okay as long as the company is earning real money and doing great work with their product or service, because if it is a penny stock or they never recover, the company may never bounce or will go to zero. So this does not always work. This is called throwing your money away because it will never bounce.

It's important to make sure you are following the steps I outlined previously in this chapter for selecting the best stocks to invest in.

This strategy has been extremely helpful to me, and I am still using it on an advanced scale right now to create solid investment strategies.

Summary

Investing is a great way to grow wealth and secure your financial future. In this chapter, we discussed a three-part strategy for making money through investing. The strategy involves investing in new technology, top business leaders, and companies that are at the top of the pack.

Dollar cost averaging is a great way to get your money to work for you. To use it to best advantage, implement the following techniques:

- **Invest in New Technology:** New technology has the potential to disrupt industries and create new markets. Investing in companies that are innovating can achieve rapid growth.

  Examples include tech giants like Apple, Amazon, and Tesla, who have created new products and services that grow and dominate.

- **Invest in Top Business Leaders:** Top business leaders often have a vision for the future and the drive to make it a reality. Investing in companies led by these leaders can provide significant returns as their vision and drive translate into success for the company.

  Examples of such leaders are Jeff Bezos, Elon Musk, and Warren Buffett, who have created and grown companies and generated wealth and changed the world.

I hope you have enjoyed this journey of learning to be a successful trader from me. If you have any questions or comments please send them to info@tradingstrategy-guides.com and use the book name as the subject line.

Thank you for reading.

Notes

1. https://www.businessinsider.com/how-old-billionaires-were-when-they-earned-their-first-billion-2016-2#evan-spiegel-25-13.

2. https://www.washingtonpost.com/archive/politics/2003/08/03/microsoft-millionaires-still-pondering-wealth/f9a55664-e695-45a5-94d5-46f4a5cefb5d/.

3. https://en.wikipedia.org/wiki/Pareto_principle.

About the Author

Casey Stubbs is the host of the popular podcast *How To Trade It*, where he shares his insights and expertise on the world of trading. In addition to his podcast, Casey is also the founder of Trading-StrategyGuides.com, a website that offers a variety of trading strategies and resources for traders of all levels, as well as his newly released proprietary trading platform, GlobalPropTrader.com. With over two decades of experience in the industry, Casey has a wealth of knowledge to share with his audience, and his podcast and website are widely considered to be among the most valuable resources for traders looking to improve their skills and increase their chances of success in the markets.

Acknowledgments

I would like to thank Wiley for giving me the opportunity to write this book. Specifically, I want to thank Tom Dinse, my editor at Wiley, and my team at Trading Strategy Guides: Ben Losier, T.J. Stubbs, and Jenn Gunter, who have helped me so much. I also want to thank my wife, Deanna, who is always so wonderfully supportive.

Index

Page numbers followed by *f* refer to figures.